Rick Steves'
RUSSIA &
THE BALTICS

Rick Steves and Ian Watson

John Muir Publications
Santa Fe, New Mexico

Other JMP travel guidebooks by Rick Steves
  Asia Through the Back Door (with Bob Effertz)
  Europe Through the Back Door
  Europe 101: History and Art for the Traveler (with Gene Openshaw)
  Mona Winks: Self-Guided Tours of Europe's Top Museums (with Gene Openshaw)
  Rick Steves' Best of Europe
  Rick Steves' France, Belgium & the Netherlands (with Steve Smith)
  Rick Steves' Germany, Austria & Switzerland
  Rick Steves' Great Britain & Ireland
  Rick Steves' Italy
  Rick Steves' Scandinavia
  Rick Steves' Spain & Portugal
  Rick Steves' Phrase Books for: French, German, Italian,
    Spanish/Portuguese, and French/German/Italian

Thanks to my hardworking team at Europe Through the Back Door, the many readers who shared tips and experiences from their travels, the many Europeans who make travel such a good living, and most of all, to my wife, Anne, for her support.

John Muir Publications, P.O. Box 613, Santa Fe, NM 87504
Copyright © 1998, 1997, 1996, 1994 by Rick Steves and Ian Watson
Maps copyright © 1998, 1997, 1996, 1994 Rick Steves' Europe Through the Back Door, Inc.
Cover copyright © 1998 by John Muir Publications
All rights reserved.

Printed in the United States of America
First printing January 1998

ISSN 1085-7230
ISBN 1-56261-389-8

For the latest on Rick's lectures, guidebooks, tours, and public television series, contact Europe Through the Back Door, Box 2009, Edmonds, WA 98020, tel. 425/771-8303, fax 425/771-0833, Web site: www.ricksteves.com, or e-mail: rick@ricksteves.com.

Europe Through the Back Door Editors Risa Laib, Rich Sorensen, Rick Steves
John Muir Publications Editors Krista Lyons-Gould, Willow Older
Research Brian Carr Smith
Production Mladen Baudrand
Design Linda Braun
Cover Design Janine Lehmann
Typesetting Kathleen Sparkes
Maps David C. Hoerlein
Printer Banta Company
Cover Photo Basil's Cathedral, Red Square; Moscow, Russia;
copyright © Blaine Harrington III

Distributed to the book trade by
Publishers Group West
Emeryville, California

While every effort has been made to provide accurate and up-to-date information, the author and publisher accept no responsibility for loss, injury, loose stools, or inconvenience sustained by any person adventurous enough to use this book.

CONTENTS

INTRODUCTION

This book breaks Russia and the Baltics into its top destinations. We focus only on Russia's two most important stops and the three Baltic capitals. For the average first visit, these five cities are the predictable and best targets. They offer a world of travel thrills with plenty of hardworking local people eager to develop their entrepreneurial skills. These vibrant, rapidly-changing cities will never be more interesting.

This book will give you all the information and opinions necessary to wring the maximum value out of your limited time and money in these top cities. If you plan two weeks or less for the Baltics and Russia, and have a normal appetite for information, this lean and mean little book is all you need. If you're a travel info fiend, this book sorts through all the superlatives and provides a handy rack upon which to hang your supplemental information.

American newspapers sometimes give an over-gloomy impression of life in Russia and the Baltic states, focusing on crime, unemployment, fuel shortages, foul-temperedness, and ominous political events. In reality, for most locals, life goes on: people buy bread, go to work a bit, ride the subway, get married, dabble in business speculation, visit their grandmothers, and grumble as much about the hardships of life now as they did about the "system" under Communism. Meanwhile, life gets better and better for tourists. Getting a visa, getting there, getting around, finding a place to stay, eating out, and meeting the locals are all markedly easier than they were even a year ago. We're not trying to convince you that Russia and the Baltics are the kind of places you should choose first for your hard-earned two-week vacation. But people who've made up their minds already, who have chosen to go and have a reason to visit—friends, relatives, business, research, study, or just curiosity—can have a great time.

Since the Baltics declared independence from the Soviet Union in 1991, travel in the Baltics has gotten more and more like travel in the rest of Europe. You don't need a visa. Well-kept restaurants and hotels offer value for your money. Just buy your plane ticket, reserve a place to stay for your first night, and go.

In Russia, because of outdated visa restrictions (more about this later), moderately-priced hotels that accept reservations in a simple and straightforward way have not developed as fast as we hoped. Planning a trip to Russia isn't *that* hard, but it's a lot different than planning a trip to Italy, and you have much less flexibility about where you can stay. So our coverage of Russia is geared to two types of people. For independent budget travelers who like the idea of staying in hostels, we show you how these safe, well-run places help you organize your trip around the two crucial practicalities: convenient visa support and an inexpensive but respectable place to stay. For those of you who already have visa support and accommodations in Russia set up (through friends, a travel agent, a package tour, or a study group), this book is useful as a concise guide to eating, sightseeing, and getting around St. Petersburg and Moscow.

This Information Is Accurate and Up-to-Date

With this book, you can travel foot-loose and fancy-free, knowing you've got good, solid information to guide you through the best of western Russia and the Baltics. Since this book is selective, covering only the cities we think make up the top two weeks, we're able to get it updated in person—visiting hotels, restaurants, and sights. You can trust that our recommendations have been field-tested. (Some publishers save money by updating their guidebooks only by letter.)

For an inexpensive, hassle-free trip, please travel with the most current edition of this book. Even with the most up-to-date edition, things change. But if you're depending on an old book for your trip, you'll learn the seriousness of your mistake . . . in Russia and the Baltics. Your trip costs about $10 per waking hour. Your time is valuable. This guidebook will save you lots of time.

Planning Your Trip

This book is organized by destinations. Each of these destinations is a mini-vacation on its own, filled with exciting sights and affordable places to stay. In each chapter, you'll find:

Planning Your Time, a suggested schedule with thoughts on how to best use your limited time.

Orientation, including tourist information, city transportation, and an easy-to-read map designed to make the text clear and your arrival smooth.

Sights with ratings: ▲▲▲—Don't miss; ▲▲—Try hard to see; ▲—Worthwhile if you can make it; No rating—Worth knowing about.

Sleeping and **Eating**, with addresses and phone numbers of our favorite budget hotels and restaurants.

And **Transportation Connections** to nearby destinations by train and bus.

The handy Appendix is a traveler's tool kit, with historic timelines, telephone tips, a climate chart, and survival phrases.

Browse through this book, choose your favorite destinations, and link them up. Then have a great trip! You'll travel like a temporary local, getting the absolute most out of every mile, minute, and dollar. Since lousy, expensive hotels are a major financial pitfall, we've worked hard to assemble the best accommodations values for each stop. You won't waste time on mediocre sights because, unlike other guidebooks, we cover only the best.

Trip Costs

Five components make up your trip costs: airfare, surface transportation, room and board, sightseeing, and shopping/entertainment/miscellany.

Airfare: Don't try to sort through the mess. Find and use a good travel agent. A basic round-trip from the U.S.A. to Moscow or St. Petersburg costs around $1,100, depending on where you fly from and when. Always consider saving time and money by flying "open-jaws" (into one city and out of another). Or fly into a cheaper European port and add Russia and the Baltics to a longer European trip. (See Itinerary Tips, below.)

Surface Transportation: For a two-week whirlwind trip of our recommended destinations, allow $200 per person for public transportation (trains and key buses).

Room and Board: You can thrive in Russia and the Baltics on $60 a day per person for room and board. A $60-a-day budget allows an average of $10 for lunch, $15 for dinner, and $35 for lodging (based on two people splitting the cost of a $70 double room that includes breakfast). Consider $70 for a double room a rough average—you could pay $20 per person for a hostel one night and $100 for a hotel room the next night. Students and tightwads travel on $40 a day ($15 to $20 per bed, $20 a day for meals and snacks). But budget sleeping and eating require the skills and information covered later in this chapter.

Sightseeing: In big cities, figure $5 to $10 per major sight (such as St. Petersburg's Hermitage), $2 for minor ones (climbing church towers), and $10 for guided walks. An overall average of $15 a day works for most. Don't skimp here. After all, this category directly powers most of the experiences all the other expenses are designed to make possible.

Shopping/Entertainment/Miscellany: This can vary from nearly nothing to a small fortune. Figure $1 per postcard, $1 per ice-cream cone, $2 per coffee and soft drink, and $10 to $30 for evening entertainment (like the ballet).

Exchange Rates

We've priced many things throughout this book in the local currency.

One U.S. dollar = approximately...

14 Estonian kroons (kr)	4 Lithuanian litas (Lt)
5 Finnish marks (mk)	6,000 Russian rubles
0.6 Latvian lats (Ls)	7 Swedish kroner (kr)

Estonia, Latvia, and Lithuania have fairly stable, permanent currencies. In Russia, the ruble's value varies considerably, so many prices are listed in Russia in dollars and then converted into rubles at that day's exchange rate. In this book, too, all Russian prices are listed in dollars, but you will always pay in rubles. Although dollars do circulate as an unofficial currency in Russia, you should politely refuse if taxi drivers or kiosk owners ask you to pay in dollars.

Prices, Times, and Discounts

I've done all that I can to ensure that the hours, prices, and telephone numbers in this book accurate. The Baltics and Russia are changing rapidly, and we know you'll understand that this, like any other guidebook, starts to yellow even before it's printed.

In the Baltics and Russia, you'll be using the 24-hour clock. After 12:00 noon, keep going—13:00, 14:00. . . . For anything over 12, subtract 12 and add p.m. (14:00 is 2:00 p.m.)

This book lists peak-season hours for sightseeing attractions (July and August). Off-season, roughly October through April, expect shorter hours, more lunchtime breaks, and fewer activities. Confirm your sightseeing plans locally, especially when traveling between October and April.

Students with International Student Identification Cards (ISIC) often get big discounts on sights—but only by asking.

When to Go

Summers are cool in the Baltics and Russia. Some days will be warm enough to wear just a T-shirt, but definitely pack a sweater for the evenings. Moscow summers bring thunderstorms like clockwork late in the afternoon. Don't trust the blue sky when you wake up; bring that umbrella. Winters are dark, cold, and dreary, and in Russia you'll still be dodging puddles of melting ice on the sidewalk as late as April. In spring and fall, too, you'll need to bundle up. See the climate chart in the Appendix for more information.

Sightseeing Priorities

Depending on the length of your trip, here are our recommended priorities.

4 days:	Tallinn and St. Petersburg
7 days, add:	Vilnius
9 days, add:	Riga
14 days, add:	Moscow, and slow down

Itinerary Tips

You can approach Russia and the Baltics from Scandinavia, Central Europe, or even China. Helsinki is the best jumping-off point: You can get to Tallinn by hydrofoil in two hours, and to St. Petersburg by rail in less than seven hours. From Stockholm you can ride the overnight ferry to Tallinn. From Warsaw you can take a ten-hour bus ride to Vilnius or a 19-hour train ride to Moscow. It may help to think of your trip as an excursion from Helsinki or Warsaw, or as an interesting way to connect Europe and Scandinavia. The Gateways chapter of this book has information on these routes.

Those doing Europe with a railpass can plan an "open-jaws" trip, using the pass in Western Europe first, finishing off with a Baltics swing, and flying home from any of the cities featured in this book.

Two weeks is plenty of time to visit the five cities covered in this book: Moscow, St. Petersburg, and Tallinn are worth three days each; Riga and Vilnius can be seen in two. This region lends itself well to overnight train or bus rides. Whenever possible, connect towns as you sleep.

Figure out where you'll start and where you'll finish. If you're visiting only Russia, it's better to go from Helsinki than from Warsaw. If you're visiting only the Baltics, either will do. Of course, you can also fly from the U.S.A. into or out of any of the cities in this book (usually with one connection).

Whatever you do, plan to make just one pass through Russia, so that you will have to get only one Russian visa. And if you have a choice, visit St. Petersburg before you go to Moscow. It's smaller, prettier, and can give you an idea whether you like Russia and really want to take the plunge and go to Moscow. Also, going from Russia to the Baltics, rather than from the Baltics to Russia, will allow you to share in the sense of liberation that Estonians, Latvians, and Lithuanians felt in 1991.

Red Tape and Business Hours

Americans need a visa to travel in Russia (but not in the Baltics). For more information, see the chapter on Getting Your Visa.

It's common for Russian shops to open on Sundays—the legacy of atheism. In the Baltics, fewer stores are open on Sundays. Especially in Russia and at state-run shops, there is an hour-long break for lunch, either 13:00 to 14:00 or 14:00 to 15:00.

Supermarkets are now common in the Baltics and are catching on in Russia. In a few stores in Russia, you might encounter the old system of having to stand in three lines: first, at the counter, to decide what you want and total up the price; second, to pay the cashier and get a slip; and third, to present the slip at the counter and get the goods. This old-fashioned system makes supermarkets feel really super.

Banking

Bring a combination of plastic, traveler's checks, and hard cash.

ATMs are proliferating in Russia and Estonia (on the street, in hotel lobbies, at metro stops), less so in Latvia and Lithuania. Bring a Visa or Mastercard with a pin number.

Exchange rates are usually pretty similar from bank to bank. Look for banks that don't charge a commission and have no more than a 1 to 1.5 percent spread between buying and selling rates. Over 2.5 to 3 percent starts to smack of tourist rip-off. In Tallinn, most banks accept traveler's checks with a minimal commission (e.g., 1 percent). In Riga, Vilnius, St. Petersburg, and particularly Moscow, fewer banks take traveler's checks, and commissions are stiffer. You can change American Express traveler's checks in all five cities covered in this book. It's possible to change cash or traveler's checks at currency exchange desks almost any time of day. You should avoid changing at "mini-market"-type kiosks or with wad-wavers on the street.

Don't bring more than half your money in traveler's checks. U.S. cash dollars are better, and you can carry them safely in a neck pouch or money belt (call us at 425/771-8303 for a free catalog/newsletter). Bring only new or nearly new currency. Worn, inky, heavily creased, or pre-1993 dollars are frequently not accepted in Russia. Carry smaller bills—a few twenties, tens, fives, and ones—since people who deal with hard currency often don't have exact change.

Language Barrier

Many young people in the Baltics and Russia have studied English and can communicate basic phrases. Particularly in Estonia, most young people speak enough to deal with basic questions, and throughout the Baltics anyone in the tourist trade will probably know some English. In Estonia and Latvia, many people over 60 speak some German. Just about everyone in the Baltics speaks Russian. Sensationalists warn that Balts will practically spit in your face if you speak Russian to them. This is true only of a tiny minority of militant nationalists. Try English first, but if you speak Russian, use it.

Latvian and Lithuanian are Baltic languages. Like Spanish and Italian, they are similar but not mutually intelligible. Russian is a Slavic language. The Slavic languages, Baltic languages, and English all descend from Indo-European. Estonian, on the other hand, is a Finno-Ugric language, completely unrelated to the others (but a lot like Finnish with the last letter of every word cut off). Look at the Estonian words for one, two, and three in the Appendix word list; the similarities and differences jump right out.

Check the Appendix for survival phrases. We've also included the Cyrillic alphabet and some pronunciation tips. Those who make a point to memorize these things will travel more easily.

Travel Smart

Upon arrival in a new town, lay the groundwork for a smooth departure. Reread this book as you travel, and take advantage of local tourist information sources. Buy a phone card and use it for reservations and confirmations. Enjoy the friendliness of the local people. Ask questions. Most locals are eager to point you in their idea of the right direction. Wear your money belt, pack a pocket-size notepad to organize your thoughts, and practice the virtue of simplicity. Those who expect to travel smart, do. Plan ahead for banking, laundry, post office chores, and picnics. To maximize rootedness, minimize one-night stands. Mix intense and relaxed periods. Every trip (and every traveler) needs at least a few slack days. Pace yourself. Assume you will return.

Pack Along

Except for a few exceptions, pack for a trip to the Baltics and Russia as you would for a trip through Western Europe.

For Yourself: Consider bringing an emergency roll of toilet paper, vitamins, and plastic bags (though you can get them on the spot, too) or a net bag.

For Gifts: Good gifts include top-quality candy and chocolate (always easy to get on the ferry from Scandinavia), well-chosen perfume or makeup, coffee, seeds (both vegetable and flower), cassette tapes, and postcards, stickers, pins, T-shirts, hats, and decals from the U.S.A. (the more Western-looking the better).

Tourist Information

The tourist information office is your best first stop in any new city. You'll find government-funded tourist offices in Tallinn, Riga, and Vilnius. In Moscow, you're on your own. In St. Petersburg a private tourist office called Ost-West Kontact Service has bravely taken on the job of giving free advice to individual tourists.

Recommended Guidebooks

You may want some supplemental travel guidebooks, especially if you're traveling beyond our recommended destinations. When you consider the improvements they'll make in your $3,000 vacation, $25 or $35 for extra maps and books is money well spent. One simple budget tip can easily save the price of an extra guidebook.

Let's Go: Eastern Europe is written by students, geared for young backpackers, and covers 17 countries, including western Russia and the Baltics. Your *Rick Steves' Russia & the*

Baltics co-author Ian Watson is a former editor of *Let's Go: Europe*.

Lonely Planet's *Russia, Ukraine, and Belarus* and *Baltic States and Kaliningrad* are good sources if you want more information on these regions, especially outside of the capital cities. *Insight Guide: Baltic States* has informative essays and good photographs, but it's too heavy to carry.

Local English-language newspapers such as the weekly *Baltic Times*, the almost-daily *Moscow Times*, and the twice-weekly *St. Petersburg Times* are a great source for the latest news, and also carry entertainment schedules.

The Baltic Revolution, by journalist Anatol Lieven, is still a good book on modern Baltic history, politics, and society. Estonia's Jaan Kross is the most widely translated Baltic author; try his short story collection *Conspiracy and Other Stories*. For Russia, no one recent commentary or history stands out as really worth buying. Instead, read one of the shorter, more digestible Russian classics, such as Turgenev's *Fathers and Sons* or Goncharov's *Oblomov*; Chekhov's plays or short stories; or even Nabokov's autobiography, *Speak, Memory*.

Rick Steves' Books and Videos

Rick Steves' Europe Through the Back Door (John Muir Publications) gives you budget travel tips on minimizing jet lag, packing light, planning your itinerary, traveling by car or train, finding budget beds without reservations, changing money, avoiding rip-offs, outsmarting thieves, hurdling the language barrier, taking great photographs, staying healthy, using bidets, and lots more. The book also includes chapters on 37 of Rick's favorite "Back Doors."

Rick Steves' Country Guides are a series of eight guidebooks covering Great Britain and Ireland; France, Belgium, and the Netherlands; Italy; Spain and Portugal; Germany, Austria, and Switzerland; Scandinavia; and Europe, just as this one covers Russia and the Baltics. If you plan to use Scandinavia as a gateway to Russia and the Baltics, *Rick Steves' Scandinavia* (John Muir Publications) is the guidebook for you.

Europe 101: History and Art for the Traveler (co-written with Gene Openshaw, John Muir Publications) gives you the story of Europe's people, history, and art. Written for smart people who were sleeping in their history and art classes before they knew they were going to Europe, *101* really helps Europe's sights come alive. (Like most European histories, it has little to say about Russia and the Baltics, but it will broaden your knowledge of Europe and give depth to your sightseeing.)

Mona Winks (also co-written with Gene Openshaw, John Muir Publications) gives you fun, easy-to-follow self-guided tours of Europe's top 20 museums (in London, Paris, Madrid, Amsterdam, Venice, Florence, and Rome).

Rick's slideshow lecture, "Scandinavia, Baltics, & Russia" is available as a two-hour videotape (call us at 425/771-8303 for our free newsletter/catalog).

Rick's television series, *Travels in Europe with Rick Steves*, is now in its fourth season with 13 new shows airing throughout the U.S.A. this year. All 52 *Travels in Europe* shows, which cover Europe from top to bottom, are aired over and over on most public television stations and most of these appear on the Travel Channel. They are also available as home videos: two or three shows per tape (specifics in our newsletter/catalog, call 425/771-8303 for a free copy).

Maps

The maps in this book, drawn by Dave Hoerlein, are concise and simple. Dave has designed them to help you locate recommended sights and places to stay. As you travel, you'll be able to find more in-depth maps at local tourist information offices or newsstands.

Maps of the Baltic capitals are easy to get in the Baltics. It may be worth picking up maps of Moscow and St. Petersburg in the West (try to get a recent map with street names in both Cyrillic and Roman) since these can be hard to find in Russia. Intourist's Roman script maps are decent ($4 at Intourist offices).

Info Off the Internet

You can now get a lot of Russia and Baltics travel information off the Web. For Russia, try starting at www.friends-partners.org/friends. A great St. Petersburg site is at www.spb.su, with links to *The St. Petersburg Press*, the city's hostels, and more. The Moscow government's official tourist site is pretty good: It's at www.moscow-guide.ru. For maps of the city center, however, go to www.moscow.net. Online copies of the unbeatable *In Your Pocket* guides to Vilnius, Kaunas, and

Riga (plus instructions for ordering the paper versions) are at www.inyourpocket.com. There's an excellent guide to Estonia (including a calendar of events and transportation timetables) at www.ciesin.ee/ESTCG. For all European rail timetables (including the Baltics and Russia), visit mercurio.iet.unipi.it.

Transportation

By Train

Overnight trains are a Russian institution. You'll board sometime in the evening, perhaps after an early dinner. Bring a late-night snack, a banana for breakfast, and enough to drink. Car doors open 20 to 30 minutes before departure. Armed with your train number, locate your platform on the announcement board in the station and show your ticket to the conductor as you step onto your car. As soon as the train is underway, she'll return to collect your ticket (giving it back before you arrive), to demand the local equivalent of a dollar or two for your clean sheets, and (in luxury compartments) to bring you tea on request. A few hours later, the lights go out and you can sleep—until you hit the border and the customs guards knock on your door.

Former Soviet sleeper compartments are among the nicest in Europe. Available only on better trains, two-bed, first-class compartments called *lyuks* or CB are an affordable luxury. Four-bed, second-class *kupe* compartments are still much roomier than Western Europe's six-bunk *couchettes*.

Departures from each city are listed in the respective chapter, and although new schedules come out annually at the end of May, year-to-year changes are minor. Still, be sure to confirm times at the station. Prices, on the other hand, are going up every month, so use the listed ones as approximations. Times are all local. Trains usually run on time. Note that in the former Soviet Union, express trains carry people almost exclusively from the first station to the last (in other words, almost everyone on a Moscow–St. Petersburg train gets on at Moscow and will get off in St. Petersburg).

Your biggest hassle will be buying tickets. There are usually separate windows for local, for national, and for international trains. And in Russia, there's an added complication: Foreigners can buy train tickets only at the special windows for foreigners—although the clerks there generally speak no language but Russian, and the tickets are the same as Russians

Major Transportation Connections

From	To (or vice versa)	Mode	Hours	US$
Helsinki	Tallinn	hydrofoil	2	$25
Helsinki	St. Petersburg	day train	7	$90
St. Petersburg	Moscow	night train	8	$35
Tallinn	St. Petersburg	night train	10	$15
Tallinn	Riga	day bus	6	$10
Riga	Vilnius	day bus	6	$10
Vilnius	Warsaw	day bus	10	$20

get but more expensive. In each city chapter, we've described the intricacies of the local system and possible solutions. There are no student discounts for foreigners.

Note that prices and policies differ from city to city, even for the same tickets on the same train. For example, a Moscow–Tallinn ticket bought in Tallinn costs less than in Moscow.

Especially in Russia, keep hassles to a minimum by handing the clerk a sheet of paper (see sample in Appendix) with your destination, date of travel, preferred train number or departure time, the number of seats you want, your desired class (write a K for four-bed *kupes*, or CB for luxury two-bed compartments), and your last name. Cheaper tickets for Π, O, or C classes are available on virtually any train. Especially on long journeys and overnight trains, avoid these cheaper classes unless you enjoy hard, non-reclining seats. The word for train station in Russia is *vokzal*.

When you get your ticket, you may have trouble deciphering it. We've included a sample train ticket for easy reference.

By Bus
The train system is still king in Russia, but buses have taken over in the Baltics. Faster and sometimes more comfortable,

Deciphering Your Train Ticket

they're now the preferred way to travel between Tallinn, Riga, Vilnius, and Warsaw. In fact the Tallinn–Riga and Tallinn–Vilnius night trains have been discontinued, and even the Tallinn–Warsaw Baltic Express is running at a loss due to lack of demand, and could be phased out. Between Russia and the Baltics, train service is running at about half of its pre-independence frequency.

Buying bus tickets is generally simple and casual, and many people just show up at the station a half-hour or hour in advance, although it's smart to reserve ahead if possible. Make sure to find out which platform your bus leaves from (it's usually written on your ticket). Your ticket will also list a seat number but only sometimes do people sit in their assigned places. Buses range from almost-new Volvos and Mercedes, through vintage Finnish hand-me-downs to wheezing Soviet relics.

The bus is worth considering for travel between Helsinki and St. Petersburg, especially for students, who get a big discount.

In Cities

Most cities are walkable. The only place where you absolutely have to take public transportation is Moscow. In every city you can buy single bus tickets (punch them on board) from kiosks or on the bus. Get Metro tokens from booths inside the entrances. Or, for a few dollars, you can buy a card good for unlimited public transportation for one calendar month.

Taxis: Taxis are still fairly cheap (but prices are rising in Moscow). In the Baltics, drivers at taxi stands may try to cheat you, or may work for private taxi companies with higher fares, so it is always sensible to call for a taxi. We've included the public taxi phone numbers for Tallinn, Riga, and Vilnius in their chapters. You may need help calling, since dispatchers' English is usually poor.

In Moscow and St. Petersburg, the way to get a taxi is just to stand by the side of the street with your hand out. Sometimes you will get an official driver with a meter, but more often a private citizen will pick you up, which is considered perfectly normal. When a car stops, open the door and state your destination in Russian, or at least some approximation of Russian. The driver may want to haggle; if he just says yes, though, keep silent about the fare until the end and then hand him a fair price. Don't be shy about refusing a ride if you don't trust the driver or if he asks too much money. Pay in local currency.

Airport buses: If you fly into Russia or the Baltics, remember: At *all* of the airports, cheap public buses stop frequently just outside the terminal exit. In the Baltics these buses run to the center of town. In Moscow and St. Petersburg they'll drop you at an outlying Metro station. Unless you're bringing barnyards of luggage, skip the airport taxi stands, where you're likely to be overcharged. (Even if you take the bus into town and then a taxi, you'll have a better chance of getting an honest deal.) You can change a little money for bus tickets in the airport terminal or with a friendly local on board.

Border Controls

Border controls between the Baltic States are quick and light, with guards hopping on board your bus to glance at your passport. Russian customs is a much more drawn-out affair with baggage declarations, searches, and an intimidating air—if you're coming by bus, you usually have to get off and line up in the customs shed. For more information, see the Getting Your Visa chapter.

Telephones and Mail

Using the telephone in the Baltics and Russia has gotten much easier. Telephone cards, which work in new digital pay phones around town, have made long-distance calls a cinch. They come in various denominations, and each country has its own cards. If you don't want to buy a phone card because you don't know how much you'll be spending on a call, head to the central post office or telephone office, where there are metered (talk now–pay later) booths. Except in Riga, local calls are free from private phones, so shops and offices will often allow you to make a quick local call if you ask politely.

Calling between Moscow and St. Petersburg costs about $1 per minute. One minute from Vilnius to St. Petersburg will run you nearly $1, and between Estonia and Lithuania calls cost about 35 cents.

The country code for Russia is 7; the city code for Moscow is 095, for St. Petersburg 812. The Baltic states have their own country codes. Estonia is 372, Latvia is 371, and Lithuania is 370. Lithuania still has city codes (Vilnius' is 2), but Estonia and Latvia are in the process of dismantling their city code systems.

From a telephone numbering perspective, the Baltic states still aren't independent if you're calling from Russia or from phones in Riga that have old numbers starting with 2. From these phones you use the old Soviet area codes (014 for Estonia, 013 for Latvia, and 012 for Lithuania) instead of 372, 371, and 370. We've included a complete dialing chart in the Appendix to help you sort things out, along with a list of international access codes and country codes.

The numbers listed in each section of this book are always the ones you dial when calling locally. See the special instructions in the Tallinn and Riga chapters on how to deal with the changing numbering systems in their countries.

Calling Home Using AT&T's USA Direct Service: AT&T offers USA Direct Service in each of the five cities in this book. These phone numbers are listed in the Appendix. Dial the local number (listed for the country you're calling from) to reach an English-speaking operator who will ask for your card number, dial your call for you, and bill your home phone number (at the rate of approximately $3 a minute plus a $2.50 service charge). Calling an answering machine is a $5.50 mistake. First use a Russian or Baltic phone card to call home for five seconds—long enough to say "call me," or to make sure an answering machine is off so you can call back, using your USA Direct number to connect with a person. Finnish and Baltic time is seven/ten hours ahead of the east/west coast of the U.S.A.; Russian time is one more hour ahead.

Avoid using USA Direct for calls between European countries; it's much cheaper to call direct by using coins, a Russian or Baltic phone card, or a metered booth in a telephone office.

Mail: The Baltic mail systems are now up to world standards (for instance, sending packages from Estonia via surface mail works great). But if you send a Christmas card from Russia, leave the year off.

Sleeping in Russia

Safe, comfortable, and competently staffed sleeping options in the range of $60 to $75 for a double room with bath have simply not developed. Clean, comfortable hotels which can issue visa support for you, like the Radisson or the Aerostar in Moscow, cost much too much—like $200 a night.

Of the precious few establishments that are both reasonably cheap and reasonably well-run, the St. Petersburg International Hostel stands out for its safety, service, and efficient visa support system. Remember, though, it's a hostel. If you don't want to share a shower with 20 people, check out the homestay options. We list reliable homestay organizations in the Getting Your Visa chapter.

Be warned that many municipal hot-water heating systems shut down for maintenance for a few weeks each summer, and entire towns (except for the very expensive hotels) go without hot water.

Sleeping in the Baltics

Finding a place to stay in the Baltics resembles finding a place to stay anywhere else in Europe, although the range of choices is a little narrower and the value-for-money ratio is perhaps a little lower.

It's possible to travel at any time of year without reservations, but given the high stakes and erratic accommodations values, we'd highly recommend calling ahead for rooms a day or two in advance as you travel. We've taken great pains to list telephone numbers with long distance instructions (see Appendix). Use the convenient telephone cards. Most hotels listed are accustomed to English-only speakers.

If you know exactly which dates you need and really want a particular place, reserve a room well in advance before you leave home. To reserve from home, call, fax, or write the hotel or hostel. Phone and fax costs are reasonable, and simple English is usually fine. To fax, use the form in the Appendix. Reconfirm your reservations a day in advance. Long distance is cheap and easy from public phone booths. Honor (or cancel by phone) your reservations.

Eating

Truly local Russian and Baltic cooking relies on bread, meat, potatoes, berries, sour cream, and northern vegetables such as cabbage, carrots, and beets, topped off with fruit compote, tea, cakes, and vodka. The best way to experience an authentic meal is on the rickety living room table in a new friend's apartment. Russians and Balts themselves almost never go out to eat, but they love having guests for dinner.

Restaurants

Russian and Baltic restaurant cooking emerged from communism ravaged and mutant. Much of what was considered best about Russian food during the Communist period actually came from more abundant areas of the Soviet Union such as Central Asia and the Caucasus (see Georgian food in the Moscow section). Amid this desolation, foreign cuisine held out the only hope of nutritional salvation. Most of the restaurants that opened shortly after the fall of Communism served Chinese, Italian, Indian, American, or vaguely international food, and eating at McDonald's felt like a square meal.

Now the tide is turning, and restaurants are proudly serving local specialities again. Try meat and vegetable pies in Russia, mushroom soup in Estonia, smoked peas with bacon in Latvia, and zeppelin dumplings in Lithuania.

Despite rising prices, you can eat a satisfying restaurant meal for $5 to $15 a person in any of the cities covered in this book. Unless the bill includes a service charge, it's common to round things up or leave a small tip (no more than 5–10 percent).

Finding good restaurants is easier in the Baltics than in Russia. Just because something says "restaurant" or "café" in Russia doesn't mean you want to eat there. Check the menu carefully. Is the restaurant clean? Is it popular with locals, tourists, anyone? For the best value, use the listings in this guidebook and the advice of your hotel or hostel manager.

When in search of a bathroom in a restaurant, remember: A downward-pointing triangle means "men," an upward-pointing triangle means "women." (Think "missionary position.")

Picnics

Small grocery stores and supermarkets have sprouted all over the Baltics and Russia in the past three to four years and buying food is no problem now. Especially in Riga and St. Petersburg, you can also head to the farmer's market for the best selection of cheese, sausage, and fresh fruits and vegetables. Russian bread is particularly good—look for the dark, heavy brown loaves which Russians call black (*chorny*, чёрный) bread. Food prices in Russia equal, and often exceed, prices in America, largely because about 60 percent of the groceries on sale in Moscow and St. Petersburg are imported. Baltic food prices are lower.

Water

If you want to stay absolutely on the safe side, drink only boiled or filtered water, soft drinks, tea, and juice. This is especially true in St. Petersburg, where a parasite called giardia infests the water system. It causes upset stomach and diarrhea, but can be eradicated with a prescription drug called Flagyl (metronidazole). Most visitors to St. Petersburg don't get sick, and if you avoid unboiled St. Petersburg water you should be OK, too. We brush with St. Petersburg water and just don't swallow.

How Do Russians Get By?

Russian salaries have not kept pace with food prices, so how do people eat? Why aren't they starving—especially the elderly, subsisting on a monthly inflation-squeezed pension check, their savings soaked away by the ruble's swift decline? This can be hard to understand on a quick visit, since you're isolated from the channels that Russians use to get by. To start with, housing and transport are subsidized, so a larger percentage of one's salary can be spent on food. Many people do part- or full-time work that doesn't show up in official salary statistics, and get extra income from renting an extra apartment or selling a car. As for the elderly, most live with extended families. When their children are at work and their grandchildren at school, pensioners have the time to shop for the cheapest (albeit lowest-quality) groceries from state-run stores, or to find the very best bargains at the farmer's markets. Many Russians are lucky enough to own or have access to a *dacha* (country home), where they spend warm weekends planting, picking, canning, and preserving fruit and vegetables to hoard through the long winters. These are their secrets of survival.

Safety and Health

Though crime has increased vastly since Communist times, Russia and the Baltics are still far safer than New York City. The situation in the Baltics is comparable to other European countries. In Russia, crime is coarser, cruder, and less professional than in America, often just a fight picked on the street or the drunken thuggery of unemployed young men. The Russian Mafia is interested in businesses and long-term residents, not tourists. Street kids can be a problem, especially at train stations and in Moscow. They'll try to reach into your pockets. Shoo them away loudly and forcefully.

Use the same precautions you would at home or anywhere else in Europe: Don't flaunt wealth, keep valuables in your money belt, avoid dark alleys, and don't talk back to drunks. Don't speak English loudly in public, and try not to draw attention to your foreignness.

Trains are generally safe, but it's wise to take some simple precautions. Women traveling by train may be able to get permission from the conductor to switch seats into a compartment with other women. You can lock the compartment door with the metal flip lock. For extra security, stuff a wad of paper, a cork, or a cut-off film canister into the cavity of the flip lock so that it can't be jimmied from the outside. Some people even tie down the door handle with a length of cord.

Ultimately, you are less at risk from criminals than from dilapidation, decay, and corrupt law enforcement. The scariest things we've had to deal with personally in Russia have been falling glass, loose manhole covers, and arbitrary cops and customs officers. The local police are not renowned for their quick response or helpfulness. (Emergency numbers in Russia and the Baltics are: 01 for fire, 02 for the police, 03 for an ambulance.)

As for health, elementary precautions are in order, but paranoia is unnecessary. Watch what you eat and drink. Avoid dubious meat and be careful about eating street food. Make

sure your shots are up to date. If you're going to be in Eastern
Europe for a few months, talk to your doctor. Take a basic
first-aid kit and any special medicines you may need. Distrust
local hospitals—if you have serious problems, consult your
embassy for a referral to a Western doctor, or head to Finland.

Surviving Russia

As conditions in the Baltic states diverge further and further
from those in Russia, it becomes more difficult to write a unified
introduction to the entire area. In 1993, when we wrote the first
edition of this book, the same advice about post-Soviet eating,
sleeping, and transportation applied regardless of whether you
were in Lithuania or Leningrad. Three years later, the Baltic
states had become "normal" European countries, and Americans
could travel from Helsinki to Warsaw without a visa, but travel
in Russia stayed substantially the same.

We face a special dilemma in writing about Russia. On the
one hand, world-famous icons of culture and history, such as
the Hermitage in St. Petersburg and the Kremlin in Moscow,
ought to be described with the reverence they deserve. On the
other, one has to admit that much of Russian life is ugly and
frustrating.

Moscow *is* one of the great cities of the world—but as
such it has more in common with Beijing and Mexico City
than with New York and Paris. By Western standards, Russia
first disappoints, then maddens, and finally saddens. Life in
Moscow and St. Petersburg is as expensive as the West and as
squalid as much of the Third World, and the weather, scenery,
and cuisine are better elsewhere.

Then why visit? Well, Russia is, in places, breathtakingly
lovely. In other places, it is awesome. (Standing in front of the
Stalin-era skyscrapers in Moscow, one cannot help but feel
both fear and respect.) And though public life on the streets in
Russia is difficult, individual people, especially inside their own
apartments, are warm and giving. In museums, churches, and
concert halls, Russia's cultural and artistic heritage survives.

And Russia is extremely important—to recent history, to
the present, and to the future of the world. It is important to
see the damage caused by the Soviets' hammer and sickle, just
as it's important to learn about the Holocaust. This is a country where millions of innocent people died under Communism,
and where the state poisoned the lives of those who survived.

Although we have listed plenty of museums and typical sightseeing attractions in this book, it would be a great waste to visit Moscow and see only the "sights" such as St. Basil's and the Kremlin. Do see the sights, but also stand in line for suburban train tickets, shop in average stores for a picnic lunch, and take the Metro during rush hour. You will get more out of your trip if you consider yourself not a tourist but a student and an explorer. Yes, you must step through puddles, avoid open manholes, crowd onto escalators, and talk to many unfriendly people through tiny holes in large windows—but it's worth it.

Stranger in a Strange Land

We travel all the way to Europe to enjoy differences—to become temporary locals. You'll experience frustrations. Certain truths that we find "God-given" or "self-evident," like cold beer, ice in drinks, bottomless cups of coffee, hot showers, body odor smelling bad, and bigger being better, are suddenly not so true. One of the benefits of travel is the eye-opening realization that there are logical, civil, and even better alternatives. A willingness to go local ensures that you'll enjoy a full dose of European hospitality.

If there is a negative aspect to the European image of Americans, it is that we are big, loud, aggressive, impolite, rich, and a bit naive. While Europeans look bemusedly at some of our Yankee excesses—and worriedly at others—they nearly always afford us individual travelers all the warmth we deserve.

Back Door Manners

While updating this book, we heard over and over again that our readers are considerate and fun to have as guests. Thank you for traveling as temporary locals who are sensitive to the culture. It's fun to follow you in our travels.

Send Us a Postcard, Drop Us a Line

If you enjoy a successful trip with the help of this book and would like to share your discoveries, please fill out and send the survey at the end of this book to us at Europe Through the Back Door, Box 2009, Edmonds, WA 98020. We personally read and value all feedback. Thanks in advance—it helps a lot.

For our latest travel information, tap into our Web site: www.ricksteves.com. Our e-mail address is rick@ricksteves.com.

Anyone is welcome to request a free issue of our Back Door quarterly newsletter.

Judging from all the positive feedback and happy postcards we receive from travelers who have used this book, it's safe to assume you're on your way to a great vacation—independent, inexpensive, and with the finesse of an experienced traveler.

From this point on, "we" (your co-authors) will shed our respective egos and become "I."

Thanks, and happy travels!

BACK DOOR TRAVEL PHILOSOPHY
As Taught in *Rick Steves' Europe Through the Back Door*

Travel is intensified living—maximum thrills per minute and one of the last great sources of legal adventure. Travel is freedom. It's recess, and we need it. Experiencing the real world requires catching it by surprise, going casual . . . "Through the Back Door."

Affording travel is a matter of priorities. (Make do with the old car.) You can travel—simply, safely, and comfortably—just about anywhere in the world for $60 a day plus transportation costs. In many ways, spending more money only builds a thicker wall between you and what you came to see. The world is a cultural carnival, and time after time, you'll find that its best acts are free and the best seats are the cheap ones.

A tight budget forces you to travel close to the ground, meeting and communicating with the people, not relying on service with a purchased smile. Never sacrifice sleep, nutrition, safety, or cleanliness in the name of budget. Simply enjoy the local-style alternatives to expensive hotels and restaurants.

Extroverts have more fun. If your trip is low on magic moments, kick yourself and make things happen. If you don't enjoy a place, maybe you don't know enough about it. Seek the truth. Recognize tourist traps. Give a culture the benefit of your open mind. See things as different, but not better or worse. Any culture has much to share.

Of course, travel, like the world, is a series of hills and valleys. Be fanatically positive and militantly optimistic. If something's not to your liking, change your liking. Travel is addicting. It can make you a happier American as well as a citizen of the world. Our Earth is home to nearly 6 billion equally important people. It's humbling to travel and find that people don't envy Americans. They like us, but with all due respect, they wouldn't trade passports.

Globe-trotting destroys ethnocentricity. It helps you understand and appreciate different cultures. Travel changes people. It broadens perspectives and teaches new ways to measure quality of life. Many travelers toss aside their hometown blinders. Their prized souvenirs are the strands of different cultures they decide to knit into their own character. The world is a cultural yarn shop. And Back Door travelers are weaving the ultimate tapestry. Come on, join in!

GETTING YOUR VISA

No More Baltic Visas

Americans no longer need a visa to enter *any* of the three
Baltic states as a tourist. Just like going to England, Italy, or
Sweden, all you need is your passport. For those who do
require a Baltic visa, such as Canadians visiting Latvia, getting
one is a simple matter of sending your passport to the nearest
consulate with a single form and a small fee. (For the Latvian
embassy in Ottawa call 613/238-6868.) Canadians enter
Lithuania and Estonia visa-free.

Russian Visas

Getting your Russian visa isn't hard, but it takes several weeks
of pre-trip planning. Not only does Russia require visas for
foreign tourists, they require you to present an official letter
from a sponsoring organization in Russia. In other words,
whereas getting a visa for most countries in the world simply
means presenting your passport at the consulate and paying for
a stamp, to visit Russia you also need to give the consulate a
"visa support letter" from a Russian organization, which tech-
nically commits that organization to taking responsibility for
you while you're in Russia. For some tourists, this organization
is the travel agency or tour operator who is arranging your
trip; for independent travelers, it is usually a hotel or hostel
where you'll be staying for part of your journey. This means
that you have a special relationship with this hotel. You're not
a free agent; you don't just call up and say "Hi, I'm coming on
the 25th." Rather, you make a commitment to them, and in
return they give you a piece of paper which makes it all OK
with the men in blue.

Getting Started

First, send a self-addressed, stamped envelope to the nearest of
the Russian consulates listed at the end of this section, with a
request for visa application forms and instructions (or use their
fax-back service at 800/634-4296). Fill out the English side of
the application. For most readers of this book, the object of
your journey will be "tourism." Under dates of travel, you
might add a few days at the beginning and the end of your trip,

just for flexibility. Leave the line about "Index and name of your tourist group" and the medical coverage line blank. Collect three passport-size photographs, and make a photocopy of the first page of your passport.

You won't need to send in your passport, because a Russian visa is not a passport stamp, but rather a piece of colored paper folded into three sections. The first section is your entry (въезд) visa, which is torn off by the border guard as you enter the country. The middle section is blank-backed for registration stamps. The last section is your exit (выезд) visa, which, together with the middle page, is taken away by the guard as you leave the country. The next step before you send in your application is to get a visa support letter.

Visa Support Sources

The **St. Petersburg International Hostel** can easily get you a visa (even if you're not staying at the hostel). See the St. Petersburg Sleeping section for more details. They take bookings for several other hostels in Russia and the Travellers Guest House in Moscow. Like most organizations, the International Hostel will give you a visa that is valid for slightly longer than you plan to stay in St. Petersburg, so that you can travel elsewhere or visit friends; however, be sure to ask them to do this.

You can also get visa support from organizations in Russia that book accommodations for you and fax you a visa support letter, then leave it to you to submit everything to the consulate. Two such organizations include: **Host Family Association,** which arranges homestays with families in St. Petersburg and Moscow for $30 per night for one person, $50 for two, or $60 single/$90 double with all the meals (tel. & fax 7/812/275-1992 in St. Petersburg, e-mail: alexei@hofak.hop.stu.neva.ru) and **White Nights,** which sets up hotels ($50–100 per room) and homestays (about $25 per person) in St. Petersburg and Moscow (Web site: www.concourse.net/bus/wnights/, e-mail: wnights@ russia.spb.su; ideally, contact Russian office via e-mail, but if you lack e-mail, contact Sacramento office at tel. & fax 916/979-9381). Another possibility is **Ost-West Kontact Service** in St. Petersburg (see St. Petersburg chapter). In theory, any Russian hotel should be able to issue you visa support, but except for the most expensive places, most are not very adept at dealing with foreigners traveling independently.

Another way to get visa support is simply to pay a Russian organization to go to the trouble of sending you a visa support letter even though you may have nothing more to do with them. **IRO Travel** in Moscow will do this for you (see the Moscow chapter). When you arrive in Russia, you'll need to have the organization that issued the letter register you with OVIR (see below). This means a trip to the organization's office and sometimes leaving your passport and visa with them for a day or two.

If you have friends in Russia, they can mail you a so-called "private" visa invitation slip that they get from their local OVIR office (see below). This serves as your visa support letter, and you should write "private visit" on your application instead of "tourism." You can also get visa support letters from Russian companies, institutions, and other organizations outside the travel industry; in this case you should probably put down "business" on your application as the purpose of your trip. Finally, if you have a cross-Russia train ticket (like on the Trans-Siberian), the ticket serves as your visa support and the purpose of your trip is "transit." Transit visas are less desirable since they limit your time in Russia.

Sending in the Visa Application

With your visa support in hand, you're almost there. Assemble your application, your three photographs, the photocopy of the front page of your passport, and your visa support letter. Make out another self-addressed, stamped envelope. Type a cover letter; it could just say "Enclosed please find all the materials for my visa application." Write a $40 check to the consulate for their standard two-week turnaround, and send everything off to them. (If you want your visa faster, they'll be happy to take more of your money.)

We're all hoping that Russia will simplify their visa requirements. There's nothing unusual about having to get special permission from a country before you're allowed to visit. But it *is* unusual to require people to get an official sponsor for their trip. It dates from an era when travelers were always affiliated with a state-run organization rather than responsible for themselves. It also encourages abuse, since independent visitors are in effect simply paying their sponsoring organization for an official letter and a signature. Unfortunately the Russian Foreign Ministry hasn't seemed to realize that the best way to reform the system is to eliminate the sponsorship and invitation requirement, at least for short visits by tourists from wealthier countries, who aren't likely to try to settle in Russia. This is the way most countries handle visas. And it would also be a big boost to the Russian travel and tourism industry. But in Russia there is a tendency for bureaucracy to be organized in exactly the opposite way from what might seem most sensible to Americans, and getting a visa is your first chance to get used to this. There may also be an element of pride involved. For a Russian, getting a Western visa is a long and humiliating process; if Russia issued visas to Westerners any more quickly, the imbalance might seem incompatible with Russia's perceived "greatness."

Notes on Russian Visas

A normal single-entry visa is valid for one entry and one exit at any time between the dates listed on it. It is possible to get multiple-entry Russian visas, but it's a lot of extra hassle and money (ask at IRO Travel in Moscow if you're serious). Instead, structure your trip so that you pass through Russia only once.

Foreigners can travel almost anywhere in Russia now, although visas still have a "destination" line which sometimes lists just one or two cities.

You can get your visa from any Russian consulate in the world. The application procedure is roughly similar, though every consulate has peculiar mutations. Also, you don't have to get your visa by mail; if you live nearby, you can just bring everything to the consulate and come back in a couple of weeks to pick up your visa.

Once you have your visa and are in Russia, you can stay at any hotel regardless of whether it is set up to offer foreigners visa support or not. For example, there are plenty of old Soviet hotels in St. Petersburg and Moscow with shoddy (but usually acceptable) rooms and high (but usually not outrageous) prices. They're rarely used to dealing with independent travelers and they aren't good at sending visa support letters overseas, but if you call up and ask for a room they will likely say yes. However, we strongly advise setting up all your Russian accommodations in advance from the United States.

Group Tours and Packages

Russia is one place where a group tour or a package can make sense. The organizers do all the hard work for you—visa processing and registration, hotel reservations, and transfers. We can recommend a tour operator, and you can ask your travel agent about others. EuroCruises offers a two-night trip to St. Petersburg, starting in Helsinki, for $525 per person including round-trip train fare, double occupancy in a good hotel, breakfasts, transfers, and sightseeing (tel. 800/688-3876). From April through mid-August, Eurocruises also makes the same trip by boat for about $560 per person (for a cabin with window).

Registering Your Visa

You'll notice that your Russian visa says "every person is required to register his passport within three days after his arrival in the destination point with the exception of holidays and days off." Only travelers on transit visas are exempt from registration.

The organization that issued your visa support letter is responsible for registration when you arrive in Russia. Make sure that the people who give you your visa support letter tell you where, when, and by whom your visa will be registered. Registration consists of a stamp on the white page of your visa by the state Visa and Registration Authority (known as OVIR, which rhymes with "severe"). OVIR permits some organizations, particularly hotels, to have their own stamps on the premises so they don't have to come to the office every day. In fact, any Russian hotel you stay in may stamp your visa even if they have no connection with your inviting organization.

Registration used to be a way of keeping tabs on visiting foreigners. But since restrictions on internal travel were eliminated in 1991, registration has become an entirely pointless bureaucratic exercise. Without going into all the gory details, let's just say that the system is too absurd and cumbersome to be perfectly comprehensible or perfectly enforceable. In practice, you should make sure that the organization that invited you registers you. Although you can try to have this done within three days of your arrival, probably no one will care if you are late. Most important, _make sure that your visa gets stamped at least once before you leave Russia._ It matters little where. Leaving Russia with an unstamped visa is a fifty-fifty proposition. They might not notice; if they do notice, they might not care; if they do care, the border guards might only extort a $50 to $200 "fine" from you, but they could prevent you from leaving the country.

Extending Your Russian Visa

Avoid extending your Russian visa. The only way to prolong your stay in Russia is to have the organization that invited you apply to OVIR for an extension, an often unsuccessful process which includes bringing your passport and writing an official letter using various stock phrases such as "The matter will be dealt with according to the established protocol." You are not allowed to deal with OVIR yourself. Rules, fees, and extension lengths differ from one OVIR to the next and from one month to the next.

Leaving Russia with an expired visa is a major sin. Don't do it. While crossing the border at 1:00 a.m. on a visa that expired at midnight may be overlooked, and one or two days' lateness could prompt a fine, anything longer than that and you may simply not be let out of the country. If this happens, it is possible to obtain a special "exit visa" from OVIR. Ask for help from the organization that originally invited you. If all else fails, contact your consulate.

Currency Declarations

When you enter Russia, you should be given a small form for declaring how much foreign currency you are carrying. Make sure that you fill out this form (it's called a *deklaratsiya* or декларация) and that it gets stamped by one of the customs officers. Keep it safe so that you can surrender it when you exit Russia. Under communism, the purpose of the declaration was to prevent you from depleting the Soviet Union's scarce foreign exchange reserves, and on leaving Russia the customs service can still confiscate currency in excess of what you declared when you entered—despite the fact that there are now ATMs in Moscow where you can withdraw money from your American bank account! One of the reasons the declarations are still in use may be to enrich the pockets of the customs officers who "fine" exiting travelers who either lost their *deklaratsiya*, or were never given one from the start.

Russian Consulates in the U.S.A.

For an application, send a SASE to the consulate. People in the know say that the Russian consulate in New York can be a stickler for details, whereas the San Francisco consulate is the most friendly and lenient.

New York: 9 E. 91st St., New York, NY 10128. This consulate, open Monday through Friday 9:30 to 12:30, has an

automated fax-on-demand number, 212/693-1358, which
spews out helpful information, including an application, if you
have a fax machine. To talk to a real person, call 212/348-0926
(fax 212/831-9162).

Washington, DC: 1825 Phelps Place NW, Washington,
DC 20008, tel. 202/939-8907, fax 202/483-7579.

Seattle: 2323 Westin Building, 2001 6th Ave. Seattle, WA
98121, tel. 206/728-1910, fax 206/728-1871.

San Francisco: 2790 Green St., San Francisco, CA 94123,
tel. 415/929-0862, fax 415/929-0306.

Russian Consulate in Helsinki
(5 mk = $1)

The Helsinki consulate is a convenient place to get your visa
processed if you're going to be spending any time in Finland.
The Russian diplomatic complex in Helsinki occupies an entire
city block next to the "Kaivopuisto" stop of trams 3B and 3T (if
you're coming south on 3B, it's the stop after the last ferry terminal). You can also walk from the center of town. The consular
entrance is at Vuorimiehenkatu 6 (tel. 09/661-449), near the
corner of Ullankatu on the other side of the complex from the
tram. By Russian standards it's extremely efficient, and English
is spoken. One-week processing costs 100 mk, two- to three-day
processing costs 300 mk, and same-day processing might be
available—ask. Show them a Trans-Siberian ticket and they'll
normally outfit you with a ten-day transit visa, which costs the
same. Standard paperwork is required (Monday–Friday 9:30–
12:00, but get there at 9:00 for a good spot in line; the sign that
says the consulate opens at 10:00 is wrong).

GATEWAYS TO RUSSIA AND THE BALTICS: HELSINKI, STOCKHOLM, AND WARSAW

Here are some tips to help you make it smoothly through the transportation and bureaucratic hoops you'll encounter if you use Helsinki, Stockholm, or Warsaw as a gateway to Russia and the Baltics.

Helsinki is just a cruise away from Stockholm. To help you out, we've included a pared-down version of the Helsinki chapter from *Rick Steves' Scandinavia*.

Sailing From Stockholm to Helsinki

The next best thing about Helsinki is getting there . . . by cruise ship from Stockholm.

Europe's most scenic cruise starts in Stockholm with lush archipelago scenery, a setting sun, and a royal

Sailing from Stockholm to Helsinki

smørgåsbord dinner. Spend the night dancing, gambling, steaming (in the sauna), and shopping with duty-free-crazy Finns and Swedes.

Two fiercely competitive cruise lines, Viking and Silja, connect the capitals of Sweden and Finland with a 14-hour cruise that leaves each port twice daily (in the morning and evening). You'll pay about $100 for the cheapest cabin and round-trip passage (Eurailers get free deck passage on Viking and discounts from Silja). Reservations are easy to make in Stockholm (Viking Line tel. 08/452-4000, Silja Line tel. 08/222-140), in Helsinki (Viking tel. 09/12351, Silja tel. 9800/74552), and in the U.S.A. (Viking tel. 800/688-3876, Silja tel. 800/323-7436).

For maximum fun and savings on hotel costs, leave Stockholm in the evening. The ship docks after a smørgåsbord breakfast and it's Hello, Helsinki.

HELSINKI

Helsinki feels close to Russia. It is. Much of it reminds me of St. Petersburg. It's no wonder Hollywood chose to film *Dr. Zhivago, Reds,* and *Gorky Park* here. (They filmed the Moscow Railway Station scenes in *Dr. Zhivago* in the low red-brick building near the Viking Terminal.) There is a huge and impressive Russian Orthodox church overlooking the harbor, a large Russian community, and several fine Russian restaurants.

In the early 1800s, the Russians took Finland from Sweden and moved the capital eastward from Turku, making Helsinki the capital of their "autonomous duchy." I asked a local woman if a particular café was made for Russian officers. She said wryly, "All of 19th-century Helsinki was made for Russian officers."

Today Helsinki is gray and green. A little windy and cold, it looks like it's stuck somewhere in the north near the Russian border. But it makes the best of its difficult situation and will leave you impressed and glad to have dropped in.

If you're arriving by boat from Stockholm, start with the two-hour "Hello, Helsinki" bus tour that meets the boat at the dock. Enjoy Helsinki's ruddy harborfront market, count goosebumps in her churches, and dive into Finnish culture in the open-air folk museum.

Helsinki

Europe's most neoclassical city has many architectural overleafs, and it tends to turn guests into fans of architecture. Its buildings, designs, fashions, and people fit sensitively into their surroundings. An architect might say, "Dissimilar elements are fused into a complex but comfortable whole." It's an intimate and human place.

Planning Your Time

Allow at least a day for Helsinki. Take the orientation bus tour upon arrival, mingle through the market, buy and eat a picnic, and drop by the TI. People-watch and browse through downtown. For the afternoon, choose between the Open-Air Folk Museum or a harbor boat tour. Relax over a cup of coffee in the Café Kappeli.

Orientation (Helsinki's tel. code: 09; from outside Finland: 358-9)

Helsinki is a colorful shopping town of 500,000 people. The compact city center is great for roaming and brisk walking.

Tourist Information: Helsinki has TIs at the boat terminals, inside the train station, and on Market Square (Market Square office open Monday–Friday 9:00–19:00, weekends 9:00–15:00, shorter hours off-season, tel. 09/169-3757 or 09/174-088, fax 09/169-3839, Web site: www.hel.fi). The TIs are uniformly friendly, helpful, well stocked in brochures, and blond(e). Pick up the city map; the "Route Map" (public transit); "Helsinki on Foot" (six well-described walking tours with maps); the monthly *Helsinki This Week* magazine that lists sights, hours, and events; and *City* magazine (good opinionated restaurant listings, geared for the younger crowd). Ask for the brochure on the scenic 3T tourist tram and go over your sightseeing plans. **Tour Expert**, a travel agency at the TI, is efficient and helpful for hotels and excursions, especially to the Baltics (same hours as TI, tel. 09/622-6990, fax 09/6226-9914).

Money Exchange: FOREX exchange desks are all over town (daily 8:00–21:00).

Telephoning: Helsinki's area code is 09 and Finland's country code is 358. When calling Helsinki from outside Finland, add the country code and drop the 0. Dial the international access code of the country you're calling from (usually 00 in Europe), then dial 358-9-local number.

Museum Pass: The **Helsinki Card** is worth considering (24 hours/105 mk, includes free entrance to sights, use of buses and trams, and a 70-mk bus tour; 48 hours for 135 mk; buy at TI).

Getting Around Helsinki

By Bus and Tram: With the public-transit route map and a little mental elbow grease, the buses and trams are easy, giving you the city by the tail. Tickets (7 mk per ride, 9 mk for an hour of travel) are purchased from the driver.

The Tourist Ticket (25 mk for 24 hours of unlimited travel) pays if you take three or more rides. The Helsinki Card (105 mk) gives you free entry to city sights and use of all buses and trams for 24 hours.

The tourist tram, 3T, makes the rounds of most of the town's major sights, letting you stop and go for 9 mk an hour. The TI has a helpful explanatory brochure (not available on the bus). Bus #24 goes farther afield but is similar to the tourist tram 3T (with great guide brochure also from TI). Each of these give you a great, cheap, go-any-time, once-over-lightly, do-it-yourself tour. In summer the red "Pub Tram" makes a 40-minute circle through the city while its passengers get looped on the (one) beer that comes with the 30-mk ticket (hourly from 11:00–15:00 and 17:00–22:00, from Mikaelsgata in front of Fennia building across from the train station).

By Bike: Citysafari rents bikes at the old market hall (near the Silja Terminal, 50 mk for two hours, 20 mk per hour thereafter, tel. 0400-50-3939). Greenbike also rents bikes (at Mannerheimintie 13, across from the Parliament House).

Do-It-Yourself "Welcome to Helsinki" Walk

Start at the harbor. The colorful **produce market** on Market Square thrives from 7:00 to 14:00 and 15:30 to 20:00 (closed Saturday afternoon and sometimes on Sunday). The head of the harbor, facing the cruise ships, is Helsinki's center. The fountain features the symbol of Helsinki, the Daughter of the Baltic. The pale blue building facing the market is the City Hall. Beyond that is the Presidential Palace. Don't miss the busy two-tone red-brick indoor market hall adjacent. Across the street you'll see the **Tourist Office**. The round door next to the TI leads into the delightful **Jugendsalen**. Designed, apparently, by a guy named Art Deco, this free and pleasant information center for locals offers interesting historical exhibits and a public WC (Monday–Friday 9:00–16:00, Pohjoisesplanadi 19).

One block inland behind the tourist office are the fine neoclassical **Senate Square** and **Lutheran Cathedral**. You'll pass the Schroder Sport Shop on Unioninkatu, with a great selection of popular Finnish-made Rapula fishing lures—ideal for the fisherfolk on your gift list.

Across the street from the TI, in the park facing the square, is my favorite café in northern Europe, **Café Kappeli**. When you've got some time, dip into this turn-of-the-century gazebo-like oasis of coffee, pastry, and relaxation. Built in the 19th century, it was a popular hangout for local intellectuals and artists. Today the café offers the romantic tourist a great 10-mk-cup-of-coffee memory (unguarded WC just inside the door).

Behind the café runs the entertaining park, sandwiched between the north and south **Esplanadi**—Helsinki's top shopping boulevard. Walk it. The north (tourist office) side is interesting for window-shopping, people-watching, and sun-worshiping. You'll pass several stores specializing in Finnish design. The huge Academic Bookstore, designed by Alvar Aalto (nearby at 1 Keskuskatu), has a great map and travel-guide section and café. Finally you'll come to the prestigious Stockman's department store—Finland's Harrods. This biggest, best, and oldest store in town has fine displays of local design. Just beyond is the main intersection in town, Esplanadi and Mannerheimintie. Nearby you'll see the famous ***Three Blacksmiths*** statue. (Locals say, "If a virgin walks by, they'll strike the anvil." It doesn't work. I tried.)

A block to the right, through a busy shopping center, is the harsh (but serene) architecture of the central **train station,** designed by Eliel Saarinen in 1916. The four people on the facade symbolize the peasant farmers with lamps coming into the Finnish capital. Wander around inside. Continuing past the Posti and the statue, return to Mannerheimintie, which leads to the large white **Finlandia Hall,** another Aalto masterpiece. While it's not normally open, there are often two tours a day in the summer (ask at the TI). Across the street is the excellent little Finnish **National Museum** (looks like a church, designed by Finland's first three great architects, closed until October 1, 1999), and a few blocks behind that is the sit-down-and-wipe-a-tear beautiful rock church, **Temppeliaukio.** Sit. Enjoy the music. It's a wonderful place to end this Welcome to Helsinki walk.

From nearby Arkadiankatu Street, bus #24 will take you to the **Sibelius Monument** in a lovely park. The same ticket is good on a later #24. Ride to the end of the line—the bridge to Seurasaari island and Finland's open-air folk museum. From here, bus #24 returns to the Esplanadi.

Sights—Helsinki
▲▲▲**Orientation Bus Tour**—A fast, very good two-hour introductory tour leaves every morning around 9:30 from both the Viking and Silja terminals after the ships dock from Stockholm. The rapid-fire two- or three-language tour costs 80 mk (120 Swedish kroner) and gives a good historic overview—a look at all the important buildings from the newly remodeled Olympic Stadium to embassy row, with too-fast ten-minute

stops at the Lutheran Cathedral, the Sibelius monument, and the Church in the Rock (Temppeliaukio). You'll learn strange facts, such as how they took down the highest steeple in town during World War II so the Soviet bombers flying in from Estonia couldn't see their target.

If you're on a tight budget and don't mind missing the more distant sights, you can do the core of this tour on your own, as explained in my city walk (above). But I thoroughly enjoyed listening to the guide. He sounded like an audio shredder that was occasionally turned off so English could come out.

If you'd like more time in the Church of the Rock, leave the tour there and consider walking 3 blocks to look at the National Museum (closed until October 1, 1999) and Finlandia Hall.

A shorter, cheaper bus tour is nearly as good (70 mk and included on the Helsinki Card, daily in summer at 11:30 and 13:30 from the train station or near the TI at 10:30 or 12:30, no stop at the Lutheran Cathedral), but I like the "pick you up at the boat and drop you at your hotel or back on Market Square" efficiency of the 9:30 tour. Buy your ticket on board or at the tourist desk in the terminal (availability is no problem).

▲▲**Lutheran Cathedral**—With its prominent green dome overlooking the city and harbor, this church is Carl Ludwig Engel's masterpiece. Open the pew gate and sit to savor neoclassical nirvana. Finished in 1852, the interior is pure architectural truth (Monday–Saturday 9:00–18:00, Sunday 12:00–16:00; off-season 10:00–16:00).

Senate Square—From the top of the steps of the Lutheran Cathedral, study Europe's finest neoclassical square. The Senate building is on your left. The small blue stone building with the slanted mansard roof in the far left corner is from 1757, one of just two pre–Russian conquest buildings remaining in Helsinki. On the right is the university building. Czar Alexander II, a friend of Finland's, is honored by the statue in the square. The huge staircase leading up to the cathedral is a popular meeting and tanning point in Helsinki. Cafe Engel is a popular hangout on the square opposite the church.

▲▲**Uspensky Russian Orthodox Cathedral**—Hovering above Market Square and facing the Lutheran Cathedral as Russian culture faces Europe's, is a fine icon experience and western Europe's largest Russian Orthodox church (built 1868, daily 9:30–16:00 except Tuesday 9:30–18:00 and Sunday 12:00–15:00).

▲▲▲**Temppeliaukio Church**—Another great piece of church architecture, this was blasted out of solid rock and capped with a copper-and-skylight dome. It's normally filled with live or recorded music and awestruck visitors. I almost cried. Another form of simple truth, it's impossible to describe. Grab a pew. Gawk upward at a 14-mile-long coil of copper ribbon. Look at the bull's-eye and ponder God. Forget your camera. Just sit in the middle, ignore the crowds, and be thankful for peace— under your feet is an air-raid shelter that can accommodate 6,000 people (Monday–Friday 10:00–20:00, Saturday 10:00–16:00, Sunday 12:00–13:45 and 15:15–17:45). To experience the church in action, attend the Lutheran English service (Sunday at 14:00, tel. 09/494-698) or one of the many concerts. You can buy individual slides or the picture book.

▲**Sibelius Monument**—Six hundred stainless-steel pipes shimmer over a rock in a park to honor Finland's greatest composer. Notice the face of Sibelius (which the artist was forced to add to silence the critics of this abstract work). Bus #24 stops here (or catch a quick glimpse on the left from the bus) on its way to the open-air folk museum. The 3T tram, which runs more frequently, stops a few blocks away. By the way, music lovers enjoy the English-language tours of the slick new Finnish National Opera (closed in June and July).

▲**Seurasaari Open-Air Folk Museum**—Inspired by Stockholm's Skansen, also on a lovely island on the edge of town, this is a collection of 100 historic buildings from every corner of Finland. It's wonderfully furnished and gives rushed visitors an opportunity to sample the far reaches of Finland without leaving the capital city. Buy the 10-mk guidebook. (The park is free, 20 mk to enter the buildings, daily June–August 11:00–17:00; late May and early September weekdays 9:00–15:00, weekends 11:00–17:00.) Off-season it's quiet. Just you, log cabins, and birch trees—almost not worth a look. In winter, the park is open but the buildings are closed. Ride bus #24 to the end and walk across the quaint footbridge. Call the museum or ask at the TI about free English tours (daily except Wednesday at 11:30 and 15:30) and evening folk-dance schedules (usually Tuesday, Thursday, and Sunday at 19:00, tel. 09/484-712).

For a 10-mk bottomless cup of coffee in a cozy-like-someone's-home setting, stop by the café near the Seurasaari Bridge, up the road at Tamminiementie 1 (June–August 11:00–23:00). Great bagels and Chopin, too.

National Museum—Museum is closed until October 1, 1999.

Finlandia Hall—Alvar Aalto's most famous building in his native Finland means little to the non-architect without a tour (20 mk, summer only, tel. 09/40241 for hours).

▲**Harbor tours**—Several boat companies line Market Square, offering 90-minute, 60-mk cruises around the waterfront nearly every hour from 10:00 to 18:00. The narration is slow-moving—often tape-recorded and in as many as four languages. But if the weather's good and you're looking for something one step above a snooze in the park, it's a nice break. If you like fish with your harbor views, IHA-Lines offers a fish buffet boat tour (70 mk, 10:30, 12:15, 14:30, 90 minutes, from the Market Square).

▲**Flea Market**—If you brake for garage sales, the Hietalahti Market, Finland's biggest flea market, is worth the 15-minute walk from the harbor (Monday–Saturday 8:00–14:00, summer evenings Monday–Friday 15:30–21:00 and some summer Sundays 10:00–16:00).

Suomenlinna—This "fortified island," a popular park with several museums, will be particularly busy in 1998 as it celebrates its 250th birthday (20-minute ferry or water-bus ride, 18 mk–25 mk round-trip, on the half-hour from Market Square, museums open 10:00–17:00 in summer).

Sauna—Finland's vaporized fountain of youth is the sauna. Public saunas are a dying breed these days, since saunas are standard equipment in nearly every Finnish apartment and home. Your boat or hotel has a sauna. Your hostel probably even has one. Saunas are generally not mixed—they usually come in pairs. You go in with a towel not to cover your body but to sit on. For hygenic reasons, it's bad style to sit directly on the wooden benches. For a real experience, ask about the Finnish Sauna Society (70 mk, bus #20 for 20 minutes in a park on the waterfront, men-only most nights, Thursday is women's night, tel. 09/678-677). For a cheap and easy public sauna, go to the Olympic swimming pool at the Olympic Stadium (12 mk, pool and sauna open Monday–Saturday 7:00–20:00, Sunday 9:00–20:00).

Concerts—Concerts in churches are heavenly. Ask at the TI and keep a lookout for posters. The Kallio Church has a magnificent new organ.

Nightlife—Remember that Finland was the first country to give women the vote. The sexes are equal in the bars and on the dance floor. Finns are easily approachable, and tourists are not a headache to the locals (as they are in places like Paris and Munich). While it's easy to make friends, anything alcoholic is very expensive. For the latest on hot night spots, read the English insert of the *City* magazine that lists the "best" of everything in Helsinki. For very cheap fun, Suomenlinna and Hietaranta beach is where the local kids hang out (and even skinny-dip) at 22:00 or 23:00. This city is one of Europe's safest after dark.

Sleeping in Helsinki
(5 mk = about $1, tel. code from outside of Finland: 358-9)
Sleep Code: **S** = Single, **D** = Double/Twin, **T** = Triple, **Q** = Quad, **b** = bathroom, **CC** = Credit Card (Visa, MasterCard, Amex).

Standard budget hotel doubles start at $100. But there are many special deals, and dorm and hostel alternatives. You have four basic budget options: cheap hostels, student dorms turned "summer hotels," plain and basic low-class hotels, or expensive business-class hotels at special summer or weekend clearance-sale rates.

Summer (mid-June–mid-August) is "off-season" in Helsinki, as are Friday, Saturday, and Sunday nights the rest of the year. You can arrive in the morning and expect to find a budget room. Two room-finding services can get you a double room in a three-star hotel with breakfast for 500 marks. This can be done by fax in advance or upon arrival. **Tour Expert** is in the harborside tourist office (see TI above, tel. 09/622-6990, fax 09/6226-9914). The **Hotellikeskus** room-finding service is in the train station (June–August Monday–Saturday 9:00–19:00, Sunday 10:00–18:00; off-season 10:00–17:00 Monday–Friday only; facing the tracks, it's on the left side, a pleasant 20-minute walk from your boat, or tram 3B from the Silja terminal, bus #13 from Viking terminal). Each charge 15 marks for the service. They know what wild bargains are available. Consider a luxury-hotel clearance deal, which may cost $20 more than the cheapies.

Sleeping in Classy "Real" Hotels
Hotel Anna, plush and very central, is one of the best values in town (Sb-350 mk-summer, 470 mk-winter, Db 470 mk-summer, 600 mk-winter, includes breakfast, CC:VMA, near Mannerheimintie and Esplanadi, a 15-minute walk from the docks, 1 Annankatu, tel. 09/616-621, fax 09/602-664).

Hotel Arthur, a five-minute walk from the train station and Senate Square, has spacious rooms (Sb-330–395 mk, Db-400–495 mk, CC:VMA, Vuorikatu 19, 00100 Helsinki, tel. 09/173-441, fax 09/626-880).

Hotel Skatta was originally for sailors. Now it's a stark but comfortable place just a block from the Viking Terminal on the harbor offering very cheap rooms in a quiet locale (23 rooms, Sb-250 mk, Db-300 mk, breakfast extra, CC:VMA, elevator, kitchenettes in each room, call long in advance to reserve, Linnankatu 3, 00160 Helsinki, tel. 09/659-233, fax 09/631-352).

Hotel Cumulus Olympia is often about the least expensive hotel in town (Db-380 mk-summer, 580 mk-winter, includes breakfast, CC:VMA, not so central but on the 3B or 1 tram line at the Sport Hall stop, 2 Lantinen Brahenkatu, tel. 09/69151, fax 09/691-5219).

Sleeping in Hostels

Eurohostel is a wonderful modern hostel located a block from the Viking terminal or a ten-minute walk from Market Square renting 250 beds (S-185 mk, D-240 mk, T-360 mk, including sheets, private lockable closets, and morning sauna; less 15 mk per person with hostel cards, breakfast-28 mk, doubles can be shared with a stranger of the same sex for 115 mk per bed, CC:VMA, handy tram stop around the corner, Linnankatu 9, 00160 Helsinki, tel. 09/622-0470, fax 09/655-044, Web site: www.eurohostel.fi). It's packed with facilities including a TV room, laundry room, a members' kitchen with a refrigerator that lets you lock up your caviar and beer, a cheap cafeteria, and plenty of good budget information on travel to Russia or the Baltics including an overnight visa service for Russia and hostel booking service.

Kallio Retkeilymaja is cozy, cheery, central, well run, and very cheap (open July–August, only 35 beds, dorm bed-70 mk, not co-ed, lockers, kitchen facilities, closed 10:00–15:00, Porthaniankatu 2, tel. 09/7099-2590). From Market Square, take the metro or tram 3T, 1, or 2 to Hakaniemi Square Market.

Olympic Stadium Hostel (Stadionin Retkeilymaja, IYHF) is big, crowded, impersonal, and a last resort. (55 mk per bed in eight- to 12-bed rooms, D-160 mk, sheets-15 mk, non members pay 15 mk extra, open all year, dorm closed daily 10:00–16:00 off-season, tel. 09/496-071.) Take tram 7A to the Olympic Stadium.

Eating in Helsinki

The best food values are, of course, the department-store cafeterias and a picnic assembled from the colorful stalls on the harbor and nearby bakery. Take advantage of the red-brick indoor market on the edge of the square. At the harbor you'll also find several local "tent" cafes and fast-food stalls and delicious fresh fish (cooked if you like), explosive little red berries, and sweet carrots. While the open-air market is the most fun, produce is cheaper in large grocery stores.

At the Eurohostel, **Café Pinja** serves decent cheap meals (the fish is better than the pepper steak). In the train station, the **Eliel Self-Service** restaurant offers reasonable midday specials in a splendid architectural setting.

In Helsinki, Russian food is an interesting option. Most popular, with meals around 100 mk, are the **Troikka** (good Russian food in a tsarific setting, Caloniukesenkatu 3, tel. 09/445-229 for reservations) and **Kasakka** (old Russian style, Meritullinkatu 13, tel. 09/135-6288). Seafood is another local specialty. Many restaurants serve daily lunch specials for around 30 mk to 40 mk.

Holvari serves tasty Finnish lunches in an art-filled setting (Yrjonkatu 15, tel. 09/642-394). **Könstan Mölja** features an all-you-can-eat lunch for 45 mk on weekdays. This family-run restaurant, decorated with old photos and farming tools, serves Finnish cooking and hearty home-baked Karelian bread (Hietalahdenkatu 14, just a couple of blocks from the flea market at the end of Bulevardi).

The Lutheran Cathedral and Academic bookstore have handy cafés. For a meal with folk music, ask at the tourist office about the dinner show at the **Seurasaari Open-Air Folk Museum.**

Transportation Connections—Helsinki

By Train

Helsinki to St. Petersburg and Moscow: Taking the train from Helsinki is a speedy option, since Finland uses the wide Russian track gauge and the wheels don't have to be changed. Helsinki's train station is right downtown, within walking distance of most ferries. There are separate windows (#14–#17) for Russian and other international trains at the end of the Helsinki train station ticket hall (Monday–Friday 8:30–17:00,

Trains Departing Helsinki

Destination	Leaves	Arrives	2nd class	1st class	Notes
St. Petersburg (Pietari)	6:30	13:30	290 mk	462 mk	Finnish *Sibelius*
St. Petersburg	15:34	23:50	288 mk	522 mk	Russian *Repin*
Moscow (Moskova)	17:26	8:38	523 mk	781 mk	Russian *Tolstoi*

Saturday–Sunday 9:00–17:00). There are two trains a day to St. Petersburg and one to Moscow. They take advance reservations at tel. 010-0128 (dialed in Finland) or 358/9/702-3411 (from elsewhere), fax 358/9/707-2111.

Going to St. Petersburg, the Finnish morning train is much nicer than the Russian afternoon train. Going to Moscow, you'll save about 30 percent by taking the ferry to Tallinn, and then the Tallinn–Moscow night train.

For general train information in Finland, call 010-0121 (costs an initial 2 mk plus 3.95 mk per minute) or 09/707-5700.

By Bus
Helsinki to St. Petersburg: While the bus is almost two hours slower than the train, it has a more convenient schedule and is cheaper, especially for students. The Helsinki bus station is across Mannerheimintie from the post office and train

Buses Departing Helsinki

Destination	Leaves	Arrives	Price	Students
St. Petersburg (Pietari)	7:15	16:05	207 mk	186 mk
"	9:00	17:50	220 mk	154 mk
"	12:00	20:45	230 mk	207 mk
"	23:00	6:40	220 mk	154 mk

station. Bookings for all buses can be made at the station or by phone (tel. 09/6136-8433, fax 09/6136-8426).

By Boat

Helsinki to Tallinn: During summer only, the fastest way to Tallinn is by **hydrofoil** (or catamaran), which takes 1.5 to 2 hours. All hydrofoils leave from the convenient Makasiiniterminaali, within walking distance from the train station and the center of Helsinki. Hydrofoil service starts sometime in April (depending on how fast the ice melts) and ends by November 1. Schedules change a lot from year to year, but in mid-summer there are as many as ten hydrofoil trips per day. The first run leaves about 7:30 and the last about 20:00, and it's just a matter of showing up at the Makasiiniterminaali and waiting for the next boat (though on the most popular departures you need to reserve a day or two in advance). Fares range from 100 mk to 160 mk one-way (no student discounts); the cheaper fares are usually on evening departures from Helsinki and morning departures from Tallinn. Tour Expert offers a round-trip to Tallinn for 270 mk with ten hours in Tallinn (located in Helsinki TI, tel. 09/622-6990, fax 09/6226-9914).

Ferries run year-round between Helsinki and Tallinn and normally take 3.5 to 4 hours. There are three to five runs a day, mostly leaving from the Länsiterminaali in Helsinki's Western Harbor. This is convenient for drivers but requires foot passengers to use public transport: bus #15 from platform 46 at Helsinki's central bus station goes direct to Länsiterminaali every 15 to 30 minutes for 9 mk. Silja Line's Tallinn ferries leave from the Olympiaterminaali. Passenger tickets start at 110 mk (student discounts available). In January and February, ice in the Gulf of Finland often slows or even stops ferry service.

You can reserve a ticket to Tallinn in four ways: by visiting any travel agency; by visiting the town offices of one of the shipping companies (open business hours only); by calling the companies' telephone reservations numbers (open a little longer) and then picking your ticket up at the port; or by going directly to the port (where ticket offices are open whenever ferries run). The ferry market between Helsinki and Tallinn is changeable, but names, office addresses, and telephone numbers of the main ferry operators are: **Tallink** (Erottajankatu 19, smørgåsbord lunch available on board hydrofoils tel. 09/2282-1277, ferries 09/2282-1211, fax 09/649-808); **Viking Line** (hydrofoils only,

Mannerheimintie 14, tel. 09/12351, fax 09/647-075); **Eestin Linjat** (ferries only, Keskuskatu 1, tel. 09/228-8544, fax 09/2288-5222); **Silja Line** (ferries only, Mannerheimintie 2, tel. 9800/74522).

In 1997 all passenger ships sailing to Tallinn arrived at the main Tallinn Reisisadam ferry terminal, except for some hydrofoils which docked at the nearby Linnahall terminal. Both terminals are within walking distance of Tallinn's Old Town.

Helsinki to Stockholm: For information on the cruise that links these two capitals, see the beginning of this chapter.

By Air
If you're 24 or under, Finnair youth fares are a good deal. A one-way flight from Helsinki to Tallinn costs $50, to Riga $125, and to Moscow $170. The Helsinki Airport buses leave regularly from the Finnair City Terminal Building next to the train station.

STOCKHOLM
In this section, only transportation connections will be covered. For detailed information on Stockholm, consider *Rick Steves' Scandinavia*.

Transportation Connections—Stockholm

By Boat
Stockholm to Tallinn: Estline's *Regina Baltica* connects Stockholm and Tallinn all year long. It sails one way one night, the other way the next night. To find out the exact schedule for the month you will be traveling, look up www.estline.ee/english/schedules.htm on the Internet. Stockholm departures are at 17:30, arriving in Tallinn at 8:30 the next morning; Tallinn departures are at 19:00, arriving in Stockholm at 9:00 (all times local; Stockholm is an hour earlier than Tallinn). Deck passage costs about $55 one-way, $80 round-trip (students with an ISIC card get about 25 percent off these fares). Cabins start at about $15 for a berth in a four-person room beneath the waterline. Fares are about 20 percent higher for Friday departures from Stockholm and Saturday departures from Tallinn. In Stockholm, reserve by calling 08/667-0001 (you can pick up the tickets at the port). Bus #41 runs between Frihamnen harbor in Stockholm, where the ferry docks, and the city center (13 kr).

You can also take an overnight ferry from Stockholm to Helsinki, then another ferry or hydrofoil from Helsinki to Tallinn. You can take either Silja Line or Viking Line from Stockholm to Helsinki, but the Silja Line terminal is right next to the Tallinn hydrofoil terminal in Helsinki. Although this route takes longer, the ships are a little more luxurious and you get to see Helsinki too. Another advantage of this approach is that railpass holders get a free or discounted trip to Helsinki.

By Air
Stockholm to Tallinn and Riga: If you're 24 or under, SAS youth fares to Tallinn and Riga are a good deal (reservable up to seven days in advance). SAS has one-way youth fares from Stockholm to Tallinn and Riga for $120 and $130, respectively. Estonian Air has comparable youth fares on its daily flights to Tallinn.

WARSAW
For information on Warsaw, try *Poland*, (Lonely Planet). Canadians need a visa for Poland (consulate in Toronto tel. 416/252-5471). Americans just need their passports.

Transportation Connections—Warsaw
Trains: International train tickets are available from the international ticket windows (Kasy Międzynarodowe) on the top floor of Warsaw's Warszawa Centralna train station. Usually at least one of the agents on duty speaks English.

Crossing the border by train: Finland, the Baltics, and Russia use the Russian railroad gauge, which is wider than that used in Poland and the rest of Europe. Since trains have to change gauges at the border, passengers either wait while new bogies (wheel assemblies) are put on their car, or move into new cars with correctly spaced wheels.

Buses: Most buses out of Warsaw leave from the Warszawa Zachodnia bus station. To reach it, take bus #127 west along al. Jerozolimskie from just outside the Warszawa Centralna train station, and get off at the last stop. Buy tickets at the "Kasa Międzynarodowa" window on the south end of the waiting hall.

By Bus
Warsaw to Vilnius: It's easiest by bus. There are four buses a day: two day-runs leaving at 8:30 and 11:00, and two over-

Between Poland and Lithuania by Rail

nights at 18:30 and 19:30. Fares were $14 to $16. All the buses
left from the main Warszawa Zachodnia (West) station except
the 11:00, which used Warszawa Wschodnia (East) station.
The trip to Vilnius takes about ten hours and usually includes
two American videos.

By Train
Warsaw to Vilnius: If you must go by train to Vilnius, the
best option is to travel to Kaunas (see below), spend the
night, then continue to Vilnius (another two hours) in the
morning. There *is* a direct Warsaw–Vilnius night train, but
since it crosses through Grodno in Belarus, you get woken up
in the middle of the night four times by customs officers and
once by bogie-changing, plus you need a Belarussian transit
visa—hassles you can do without.

    Warsaw to Kaunas, Riga, and Tallinn: The Baltic
Express (the Warsaw–Tallinn train) leaves Warsaw at 14:30

daily, arriving in Kaunas at 23:51, Riga at 5:00 the next day, and Tallinn at 12:15. At 22:00, just after crossing the border into Lithuania, you have to move into new carriages (which use the wider Russian railway gauge) at the Šeštokai station. Warsaw–Tallinn tickets cost about $51 for second class, $82 for first class.

There's also direct daily overnight bus service from Warsaw to Riga for about $20, leaving at 13:00 and arriving in Riga at 3:00 in the morning.

Warsaw to Moscow: The *Polonez* train leaves Warsaw every afternoon at 14:12 and arrives in Moscow the following day at 11:58. A second-class (three-bed) sleeping berth costs about $70; a first-class (two-bed) berth about $110. Your Russian visa will be valid for transit across Belarus. Several other trains make the run from Warsaw to Moscow on their way from Berlin, Prague, and the like, but since the Polonez originates in Warsaw, the cars will be cleaner and the conductors less sleepy when you board.

Warsaw to St. Petersburg: While there's a daily train from Warsaw to St. Petersburg (the distance and cost are almost the same as to Moscow), these trains pass through Belarus, Lithuania, and Latvia on the way. According to the Belarussian consulate in New York, if you have a valid Russian visa it will be accepted for transit across Belarus on this train, but do confirm this before you go (see below). It is normal procedure for the Belarussian border control to take the first page of your Russian visa. Frankly, because of all the border checks it makes more sense to fly from Warsaw to St. Petersburg, or to go by train via Moscow.

Belarussian Visas: If you simply *must* take one of the direct trains between Warsaw and Vilnius, it is possible to get a Belarussian transit visa from the consulate in Warsaw (Atenska ul. 67, tel. 617-3212) or in Vilnius (Muitines gatve 41, tel. 630-626) for about $30 (same- or next-day processing). You need to show them your ticket. We've heard that it's still possible to get the transit visa at the border for $45 plus a lot of annoyance. Since the very existence of Belarus as a separate country is in doubt given their recent union agreement with Russia, if you are planning to cross Belarus, we suggest you confirm the regulations with the Belarussian embassy (1619 New Hampshire Ave. NW, Washington, DC 20009, tel. 202/986-1604, or the consulate at 708 3rd Ave., 21st floor, New York, NY 10017, tel. 212/682-5392).

MOSCOW

Moscow encapsulates all that's good and all that's bad about Russia. Like the country, its vast size threatens to overwhelm you and swallow you up. You feel small under the press of its weighty buildings, starchy food, and pollution. Among the sprawling tenement buildings and "Stalin Gothic" skyscrapers one can still find brilliant golden domes and reminders of Czarist days. But the Soviet penchant for gigantism forces the visitor to search out these glimpses of Russia's past like flowers in a field of tall grass.

Moscow lacks the beauty of St. Petersburg, but makes up for it in intensity. Some days Moscow will leave you mentally and physically exhausted, wondering why you decided to go there and when the plane is leaving. Other days, though, you almost like it.

The city is huge. Rides around the center can take an hour. And the contradictions that pervade its society take you on an emotional roller coaster. Russians will bump, shove, and yell at you in a bakery line, and then smile and offer you everything they have in their kitchen when you dine at their apartments. The cramped and crumbling apartments constructed by Brezhnev make the simplest church seem incredibly beautiful. A clean-up campaign has left the city virtually free of litter, yet it's hard to find a trash can. Moscow's stunning young men and women dress in the latest Italian fashion while pensioners and government workers struggle to get by. The nouveau riche streak around in mud-splattered Mercedes and BMWs, while

young mothers stand alongside *babushki* selling everything
from dried fish to a used pair of boots. The private sector is
providing an increasing number of entry- and mid-level jobs,
but for many Russians life is still a game of survival. During
these times of awkward steps towards a market economy, the
rules seem to change every day.

Russophiles are evenly split between those who prefer
Moscow and those who would choose nowhere else but St.
Petersburg. Regardless of how or whether it charms you,
Moscow is an exciting city to visit.

Planning Your Time

Plan on at least two days in Moscow. For a good visit, try this
schedule:

Day 1

10:00   Arrive in Red Square by Metro, see St. Basil's, visit
        Lenin, and wander through the GUM department
        store.
13:00   Grab a quick lunch inside GUM or at Kombi's.
14:00   Depending on the weather and your interests, head to
        the Izmailovskii Park flea market, Tretyakov Gallery,
        Novodevichi cemetery and convent, or "any random
        metro neighborhood" (explained under Sights, below).
18:00   Return to the center for dinner at Patio Pizza.

Day 2

10:00   Tour the Kremlin.
11:30   Walk along Volkhonka past the Pushkin Museum and
        Church of Christ the Savior, then cut up along the
        Boulevard Ring to the Arbat. Break for lunch at the
        Georgian restaurant on the Arbat.
15:00   Stroll down the Arbat and then return to the center
        along the almost-parallel Novii Arbat.
18:00   Walk or take the subway up ulitsa Tverskaya to
        Mayakovskaya Metro station for dinner at one of the
        nearby restaurants.

Orientation

Moscow is enormous and daunting to the uninitiated. The city
is organized in concentric circles. The outer ring road marks
the city limits while most of the important sights are contained

Moscow

within the inner Garden Ring or the innermost Boulevard Ring. At the bull's-eye are the Kremlin and Red Square. The Moscow River cuts an arc through the center of the city, with its peak touching the Kremlin.

Tourist Information: There's no central tourist office. One way to get acquainted with the city is on one of Intourist's efficient, reasonably priced, half-day tours which leave daily at

14:30 from the tall Hotel Intourist on Tverskaya, near the Kremlin ($10). If your tour includes Moscow University, you'll get a great panoramic view of the city. Marlis Travel offers city walking tours ($15 for three hours, Kronshtadtsky 43a, tel. 453-4368).

Visa Support: If **IRO Travel** has provided you with visa support, drop by to register (Komsomolskii Prospekt 13, tel. 234-6555, visa support tel. 234-6553, fax 234-6556, e-mail: visa@iro.lz.space.ru). The cheapest invitation, for a 25-day tourist visa, costs $40. A one-year multi-entry visa invitation costs $325. Contact IRO from anywhere in the world by fax or e-mail with your full name, citizenship, passport number, birthdate, and city where you plan to apply for the visa. They ask for prepayment by credit card and you can pay by fax. Though IRO Travel is affiliated with Travellers Guest House, it provides visa support regardless of where you intend to stay.

American Embassy: Novinskii/Новиский bulvar 19/23, tel. 252-2451. Metro: Barrikadnaya/Баррикадная.

News: The excellent English-language *Moscow Times*, which comes out Tuesday through Saturday, will keep you up to date on events in the capital and elsewhere in Russia. It's free at many stores, restaurants, and hotels.

Bookstores: The most convenient is **Zwemmers**, which has a modest stock of art books and fiction shipped in from England (Monday–Saturday 10:00–19:00, Kuznetskii Most/ Кузнецкий station, tel. 928-2021). Less accessibly, a few tiny one-room bookstores have opened around 1st Novokuznet-skaya pereulok 5, between Paveletskaya and Novokuznetskaya Metro stations.

Currency Exchange
6,000 rubles = about $1

Every neighborhood, often every block, sometimes every store has its own Обмен Валюты (currency exchange) desk, usually run by a bank. Little offices—even the exchange shacks inside shops—give better rates than desks in major hotels. Most banks now change traveler's checks (a commission of 3 percent on traveler's checks is a good deal here), but it's even better to bring cash and an ATM card with a pin number. ATMs are easy to find.

The Moscow branch of American Express is a little out of the way and you should try to do your banking elsewhere, but it does provide the usual menu of services. If you lose your card or checks and have to go to American Express, exit the Mayakovskaya/Маяковская Metro station and cross the street to the tower with the blue clock on it, then walk about 3 blocks along the Ring (Monday–Friday 9:00–19:00, Saturday 9:00–14:00, ulitsa Sadovaya-Kudrinskaya/Садовая-Кудринская 21a, tel. 755-9000).

Telephones and Mail

For local calls you can use almost any public pay phone (there's no difference between a Таксофон and a Телефон). They have been converted to take small brown plastic tokens sold at Metro entrances for 30 cents. Many pay phones are out of order. Lift the receiver, listen for the dial tone, dial, and wait for an answer before you put in your token.

You can do it all, from mailing a postcard to placing a call, at the Central Telegraph Office (ulitsa Tverskaya/Тверская 7, Metro: Okhotnii Ryad/Охотный Ряд). For long-distance calls within the former U.S.S.R., go to the little room to the left in the vestibule (daily 7:00–22:00). Pay first, then you can call. Rates have risen dramatically (about $1 per minute to St. Petersburg). You can also use a private phone or go to any local post office.

The post office hall is on the right as you enter the Central Telegraph Office (windows open daily 8:00–21:30, lunch break daily 14:00–15:00). If you want to send a postcard, go to the window in the back left corner of the hall to buy stamps, then put your card in one of the boxes in the vestibule. It will take anywhere from a week to two months. A better bet for value and speed is Global Sprint Fax. Go to window #13 on the left-hand side. You leave your document; they scan it and it's computer-sent; they notify you by phone if it fails to go through. One page to the U.S. or Western Europe costs about $2.50.

Getting Around Moscow

Get used to the Metro. The stops (identifiable by a glowing red M) are never much more than a ten-minute walk away inside the Garden Ring road. If you don't see one, just ask any passerby "Gdye stantsiya Metro?" (or show them this: Где станция метро?) and you will likely be answered by *"Vot"* and an outstretched arm pointing the way.

Tokens for the Metro (currently 30 cents apiece) are available from windows inside each station entrance. The latest

Moscow Metro

Within the map:

GREEN **2** **8** GREY **5** ORANGE **1** RED

6 PINK

МАЯКОВ-СКАЯ

МЕНДЕЛЕЕВ- РИЖСКАЯ

ПРОСПЕКТ МИРА

БЕЛОРУС-СКАЯ
ЦВ
НОВОСЛОБОД-СКАЯ
СУХ. КОМСОМОЛЬСКАЯ **3** DARK BLUE

БАРРИКАДНАЯ
МАЯКОВ-СКАЯ
ТУРГЕНЕВ-СКАЯ
КРАСНЫЕ ВОРОТА

КРАСНОПРЕ-СНЕНСКАЯ
ЛУБЯНКА
ЧИСТЫЕ ПРУДЫ

LIGHT BLUE **3ᴬ**
ПУШКИН-СКАЯ
КУЗНЕЦКИЙ МОСТ
YELLOW **7**

КИЕВСКАЯ
ЧЕХОВ-СКАЯ
ТВЕР-СКАЯ
КУРСКАЯ **4** BROWN

СМОЛЕНСКАЯ
ОХОТНЫЙ РЯД
ТЕАТРАЛЬНАЯ
КИТАЙ-ГОРОД

АЛЕКСАНДРОВ-СКИЙ САД
ПЛОЩАДЬ РЕВ.

АРБАТСКАЯ
БОРОВИЦ-КАЯ
ТРЕТЬЯКОВ-СКАЯ МАРКСИСТСКАЯ

КРОПОТКИНСКАЯ
ТАГАНСКАЯ

ПАРК КУЛЬТУРЫ
БИБ. ЛЕНИНА
НОВОКУЗНЕЦКАЯ

ПОЛЯНКА

4 BROWN
ДОБРЫНИН-СКАЯ
ПАВЕЛЕЦ-СКАЯ

1 RED
ОКТЯБР-ЬСКАЯ
СЕРПУХОВ-СКАЯ
PINK **6**

ТУЛЬ-СКАЯ

5 ORANGE   GREY **8**   **2** GREEN   DCH

- TRANSFER STATIONS

NOTE: NAMES GIVEN HERE IN CYRILLIC. FOR ROMANIZED NAMES SEE MOSCOW CITY MAP

—ESSENTIAL METRO WORDS—
• ENTRANCE – ВХОД   • TRANSFER – ПЕРЕХОД
• EXIT (TO CITY)–ВЫХОД (В ГОРОД)   • WHERE IS...–ГДЕ...

price should be posted near the ticket window. Go to the window, hold up the requisite number of fingers and say the number of tokens you want. For trams and buses you need to buy tickets which the drivers sell in strips of ten. They're also sold in and around Metro ticket windows.

To flag down a taxi, stand by the side of the street with your hand out. Either a taxi or private car will stop to pick you up. (You're free to accept or decline.) A ride within the center of town should not cost more than the local equivalent of $6, and rides out to the suburbs shouldn't be more than $10. Pay in local currency (rather than dollars).

Sights—The Very Center

▲▲▲**Red Square**—Any tour of Moscow should begin on Red Square in front of St. Basil's Cathedral. Surrounded on one side by the Kremlin walls and Lenin's Mausoleum and on the other by GUM, the largest department store in the country, you'll rightly feel at the administrative heart of a grand empire. It's even better at night when the square is empty, St. Basil's is illuminated, and red stars glow atop the Kremlin.

▲▲**Lenin's Mausoleum**—Though there is no longer any ceremonial changing of the guard in front of the mausoleum, you can go inside for free and decide for yourself whether Lenin is wax or flesh (Tuesday, Wednesday, Thursday, Saturday, and Sunday, 10:00–13:00). Large bags and cameras must be checked in the cloakroom on the side of the maroon-colored, closed Historical Museum. There's talk of burying Lenin in the family plot in St. Petersburg in '98.

▲**St. Basil's Cathedral**—Red Square's top ornament is St. Basil's Cathedral. Now more of a plain museum with some old icons and a barren maze of rooms than a living church, its exterior is far more interesting than its interior. Even so, after you've given the outside a 360-degree marvel, consider peeking inside.

▲▲**GUM** (ГУМ)—Once the best-stocked department store in the Soviet Union, it's now Russia's classiest mall (daily 8:00–21:00). Since 1992, hard-currency stores such as Benetton, Galeries Lafayette, and Samsonite have taken over more and more space in GUM. There are three corridors; enter at either end. Climb up to the top floor at either end of the building where there are no stores and treat yourself to a spectacular view and an amazing vantage point for photographing Russians as they go about their shopping unawares. The natural light from the skylights is especially pretty on bright days. There's a fast-food chicken restaurant and a stand-up pizza joint inside.

▲▲▲**The Kremlin**—A must-see, the Kremlin is a walled enclosure containing Russia's top government offices, as well as several beautiful Orthodox churches. The entrance is through Alexandrovskii Sad (Alexander's Garden); from Red Square, walk north past the mausoleum out of the square, go left into the garden and past the Tomb of the Unknown Soldier, and you'll come to the white Kremlin entrance tower, across from the Alexandrovskii Sad/Александровский Сад Metro exit. Ticket booths are beside the tower. You have to check your bags at the little office under the stairs (20 cents).

The Kremlin is open Friday through Wednesday from 10:00 to 17:00 (ticket office closes from 13:00–14:00 and at 16:45; closed Thursday and during frequent official functions).

Central Moscow

Entry to the Kremlin grounds costs only 30 cents, and lets you walk around the grounds, scan the Moscow River from the park along the south wall, pat the huge cannon and broken bell, and admire the church-domes, towers, and congress buildings. Entrance to the four churches costs $6 per church (students half-price). You don't have to see all four churches, and you can pay at the church door after you've peered inside and decided. Getting into the Armory costs $14 (students half-price).

On summer mornings, watch for newlywed brides and grooms who come to lay flowers at the Tomb of the Unknown Soldier back in Alexandrovskii Sad.

Sights—Downtown Moscow

Most of the following sights are on three streets that radiate from Red Square: Volkhonka, the Arbat, and Tverskaya.

▲▲**The Arbat** (Арбат)—Once a prestigious address for

Russia's eminent writers, this pedestrian street not only retains some of its original grandeur but also has the city's best concentration of kitschy tourist shops and (in summer) outdoor cafés. McDonald's graces its far end.

You can walk to the Arbat from the Kremlin entrance, going past the Lenin Library down ulitsa Vozdvizhenka/ Воздвиженка, or along the Boulevard Ring from Kropotkinskaya Metro and the Church of Christ the Savior. The closest Metro is the Arbatskaya/Арбатская station on the light blue line, directly across from the beginning of the Arbat—go through the underground passage full of middle-aged women selling puppies and kittens while artists offer to sketch you. The Arbatskaya station on the dark blue line is also convenient: exit, turn left, and walk through the crowds for about 250 meters. The Smolenskaya/Смоленская station on the dark blue line is at the Arbat's outer end.

Novii Arbat, just north of and nearly parallel to the Arbat, was built in the 1960s, and the huge apartment buildings that line it like so many open books were intended as a showpiece of Soviet success. It's now one of Moscow's most important modern shopping streets. If you want to see the **White House** (Белый Дом), the scene of the October 1993 shelling which finished the standoff between Boris Yeltsin and his hard-line foes in the Russian parliament, you can continue all the way down the Novii Arbat to the river (taking the Metro to Krasnopresnenskaya/Краснопресненская on the Ring line or Smolenskaya/ Смоленская on the light blue line will get you part of the way).

▲**Pushkin Museum** (Музей им. Пушкина)—The museum is less remarkable for its standing collections (roomfuls of paintings by Monet, Renoir, van Gogh, Rembrandt, and Picasso) than for its temporary shows, such as the Trojan Gold ($8, students $4, Tuesday–Sunday 10:00–18:00). The Pushkin Museum and Church of Christ the Savior (below) are within a couple blocks of each other (and Red Square) on Ulitsa Volkhonka/Волхонка, which runs away from the Kremlin from the southern end of Alexandrovskii Sad and the southwest corner of the Kremlin itself.

▲▲**Church of Christ the Savior** (Храм Христа Спасителя)— Originally built here in the 19th century, the church was torn down under Stalin, and a monstrous Palace of Soviets with a towering statue of Lenin was planned. When the ground proved too soft, the site was turned into a public swimming pool, demolished in 1994–95. Until the church opens, a temporary exhibit allows you to watch its reconstruction, see plans and a scale model, and learn about the history of the site (free, Monday–Friday 10:00–18:00, weekends 10:00–16:00). Across the street is the Boulevard Ring—along which it's a ten- to 15-minute walk to the Arbat—and the Kropotkinskaya/Кропоткинская Metro station.

▲▲**Ulitsa Tverskaya** (Тверская)—This is Moscow's most prestigious street. Don't miss the walk south down Tverskaya from Mayakovskaya or Pushkinskaya Metro stops to the Kremlin. You'll pass the Tchaikovskii concert hall, the original Moscow McDonald's and many more upscale restaurants, the city hall and mounted statue of Yuri Dolgoruki (founder of Moscow), the Central Telegraph Office, the Intourist Hotel, and finally the National Hotel at the corner across from the Kremlin.

▲**Tretyakov Gallery**—To get to the Tretyakov Gallery, which has the world's best collection of Russian icons and a selection of 18th- and 19th-century art (especially portraiture), take the orange line Metro to Tretyakovskaya/Третьяковская (don't go out through the connected Novokuznetskaya station, which will leave you several blocks away). Turn left at the top of the stairs, cross the street, and walk down the brick road about 100 meters to the large red-and-white building on the right ($8, students half-price, Tuesday–Sunday 10:00–20:00, ticket windows close at 18:30, closed Monday).

Sights—Outer Moscow

▲▲**Izmailovskii Park weekend flea market**—This is the place to buy your souvenirs. Most often you are dealing with the original artists, and bargaining is a must. Pick up a 13-piece *matryoshka* doll, beautifully hand-carved chess sets, Russian medals, scarves, and patchwork quilts. To get to the market, take the dark blue Metro line four stops northeast of the Ring line to Izmailovskii Park/Измайловский Парк—it's the station with a third track in the middle. Exit, turn left, and walk past the huge hotel toward the stadium and smokestacks in the distance. Notice the Intourist propaganda posters on the right along the way. (Open only on weekends and holidays, from morning till evening.)

▲**All-Russian Exhibition Center** (VDNKh/ВДНХ)—Once the Exhibit of the People's Economic Achievements, this center was a temple to the proletariat. Built in the 1930s, its 72

Neoclassical pavilions glorify Pig Husbandry, Standardization, Atomic Energy, and other giddy arts. Today it's hard to believe VDNKh was ever anything but a mall waiting to happen. Electronics is the name of the game, and every single structure has been transformed into a rabbit-hutch of cut-rate consumerism. Fascinating. VDNKh is located on Prospekt Mira opposite the Kosmos Hotel (concessions open 10:00–18:00, near Metro: VDNKh/ВДНХ).

▲▲**Any random Metro station**—To get a real feel for Russian life, try taking the Metro to any of the stations outside Moscow's Ring line. You can pick one at random, but here are some recommendations. For true Soviet residential bleakness it is hard to beat Yasenevo/Ясенево or Konkovo/Коньково, south on the orange line. If you prefer your bleakness dirty and industrial, head to the southeast, Moscow's most polluted region: Volgogradskii Prospekt/Волгоградский Проспект and Tekstilshchiki/Текстильщики on the pink line. A more desirable neighborhood surrounds the Krylatskoe/Крылатское station at the end of the light blue line in the west of Moscow. Here the prevailing west winds are still unpolluted by the city's factories, and the 18-story tower blocks were built only recently. In another well-regarded neighborhood, around Sokol/Сокол to the north on the green line, you can see Stalin-era buildings from the forties and fifties. In each case, check out the stores that Russians shop in as they walk from the Metro exit to their apartments after work each day.

Enjoy the Metro on your way. The most beautiful station is Mayakovskaya/Маяковская on the green line (don't miss the ceiling mosaics). Ploshchad Revolyutsii/Площадь Революции has arresting socialist-realist statues. The grandest stations are on the Ring line and the dark blue line.

▲**Novodevichi Cemetery** (Новодевичье Кладбище) **and Convent**—The walled convent, with its churches and graves, is one of the most peaceful places to escape to on a nice day in Moscow. Entrance to the grounds is usually free; if you want to see the museums inside you'll pay $5 (Wednesday–Monday 10:00–17:00, closed Tuesday and the first Monday of each month). The cemetery, adjacent to the convent but with a separate entrance, contains the graves of Chekhov, Gogol, Bulgakov, Mayakovsky, Eisenstein, Shostakovich, Scriabin, Khrushchev, Molotov, Gromyko, and Stalin's wife, among others. It's one of the few major attractions in Moscow without a separate price for foreigners: entrance costs $2 for everyone (daily 10:00–18:00). Ask them for their English map ($2). To reach the complex, take the red line Metro two stops southeast of the Ring to Sportivnaya/Спортивная, go out the exit towards the center, turn right and walk about 4 blocks along ulitsa 10-letiya Oktyabrya, and you'll see the spires of the convent across the street to your left. The cemetery is past the convent to your left.

▲**Gorky Park** (Парк Горкого)—Perhaps the best reason to go is the view from atop the enormous rickety Ferris wheel in the center of the 300-acre park (daily 9:00–22:30). To get to the park, take the Metro to the Oktyabrskaya/Октябрьская Ring line station, exit to the street through the right-hand doors, go left around the corner, and walk alongside the park's fence about 400 meters to the huge colonnaded entrance. Tickets are sold at the windows to the left and right for a few cents. Consider going back downtown on a riverboat, which you can catch at the terminal on the river side of the park.

▲**Sergiev Posad** (Сергиев Посад)—Formerly called Zagorsk, this is a living medieval monastery 60 km outside of Moscow (Tuesday–Sunday 10:00–18:00, closed Monday). This world of onion domes and icons, one of the most beautiful churches in all Russia, is 90 minutes by local train from Moscow's Yaroslavskii Station (Metro: Komsomolskaya/Комсомольская). Coming out of the Metro, go in the glassed-in building under the large МОСКВА sign and buy an eight-zone *obratny* (return) ticket from any of the ticket windows (about $3), then hop on any of the trains marked Sergiev Posad or Aleksandrov (Александров), which leave every hour.

Classical Music or Ballet

Scout out posters and ask at your hotel or hostel for advice on music, opera, and ballet performances. In contrast to the cleaned-up situation in St. Petersburg, getting into the Bolshoi Ballet still usually requires paying scalpers these days (the going rate is about $20), but you can try at the ticket office across the square from the theater, next to the Teatralnaya/Театральная Metro entrance, between 12:00 and 18:00. Opera and ballet in the Palace of Congresses, inside the Kremlin, is also an option; tickets are cheaper and scalpers usually don't bother with them. The ticket office (open 12:00–14:00 and 15:00–19:00) is kitty-corner from the Kremlin entrance, to the left if you stand with your back to the tower. Intourist agencies can also book tickets for $20 to $55.

From mid-September through mid-June, you can hear great classical concerts for pennies at the Tchaikovskii Concert Hall at Metro: Mayakovskaya/Маяковская, or in the two halls of the Tchaikovskii Conservatory about 3 blocks along Bolshaya Nikitskaya ulitsa from the Kremlin (on the left). Look in the *Moscow Times* for listings and stop by for tickets a day or so in advance. Most concerts and performances start at 19:00.

Sleeping in Moscow

(If calling from the U.S., dial 011-7-095, then the local number; for more phone info, see the Appendix: Dialing Direct Within Russia & the Baltics.)

Your options are still limited, but accommodations have improved in Moscow over the years. For a mid-range hotel, the Gamma-Delta is decent. Seriously consider the homestay organizations: White Nights and Host Family Association. Of the hostels, Heritage is far better (if you speak Russian or don't mind a language barrier) than Travellers Guest House (which is pricier, less comfortable, and in an ugly neighborhood, but does have English-speaking staff).

White Nights sets up hotels ($50–100 per room) and homestays (about $25 per person) in Moscow and St. Petersburg (Web site: www.concourse.net/bus/wnights/, e-mail: wnights@russia.spb.su). If possible, contact the Russian office via e-mail, but if you lack e-mail access, call the Sacramento office (tel. & fax 916/979-9381). They provide visa support (and can also book Trans-Siberian tickets).

Host Family Association, also arranges homestays in Moscow and St. Petersburg as well as the Baltic capitals ($30 for one person, $50 for two, or $60 single/$90 double with all meals, tel. & fax 7/812/275-1992 in St. Petersburg, e-mail: alexei@hofak.hop.stu.neva.ru.

Heritage Hostel, Moscow's newest hostel, is run by friendly Russian-speaking staff. They'll give you blank stares as you speak space-alien English, but they take you in like a lost child and mother you. Book through English-speaking AZ Tours (see below). Rooms are comfortable and some have fridges, TVs, and phones (dorm bed-$10, Sb-$35, D-$34, Db-$52, hostel members get $2 discount, breakfast-$2, visa registration-$3, rooms in the back overlook a park, Kos-monavtov/Космонавтов ulitsa 2, near VDNKh, Metro: VDNKh/ВДНХ, tel. 975-3501). Contact the hostel through AZ Tours, which provides visa support and registration (fax 975-3619, e-mail: evgen@az-tour.msk.ru). From the VDNKh/ВДНХ Metro stop, take the underpass to Cosmos Hotel. The hostel is across the street, set off the road in the brick building with the "АВИА" sign on the roof.

Izmailovo Gamma-Delta Hotel, part of the complex used to house athletes during the 1980 Olympics, is a clean and stress-free three-star hotel. The spacious rooms, with worn but comfortable furniture, have TVs, phones, and 24-hour hot water (Sb-$40, Db-$44, includes breakfast, ask for view room, Izmailovskoe shosse 71, Metro: Izmailovskii Park/Измайловский Парк, next to park and flea market, five stops from Red Square, tel. 166-2236 or 166-4127, fax 166-7486; communication best by fax). The Intourist office in the lobby books city tours, sells ballet and concert tickets, and says they provide visa support services by fax (though the St. Petersburg International Hostel seems a surer bet for your visa support letter).

Travellers Guest House has been Moscow's main youth hostel for the past few years, although it's not as clean or well-run as the St. Petersburg hostel. It occupies two floors of a typical Soviet student dormitory, in which every two rooms share an entranceway and bathroom. A bed in a five-bed room costs $18, while a double costs $48 and a single goes for $36. The hot water goes off for a few weeks every summer. The clientele is heavily American and British. Reserve early (Bolshaya Pereyaslavskaya/Большая Переяславская ulitsa 50, tenth floor, tel. 971-4059, fax 280-7686, e-mail: tgh@glas.apc.org). It's in a ugly, step-over-the-syringe neighborhood about a 15-minute walk from Metro: Prospekt Mira/Проспект мира. From the Metro stop, walk north about 3 blocks, turn right along the street with the four smokestacks in the distance, walk 1 block to the end of the street, turn left, and the guest house is in the tall white building on your right with red signs on the left side of the door. Take the elevator up to the tenth floor.

Travellers Guest House has an in-house student travel agency called **STAR Travel,** affiliated with Council Travel, which helps youths (under age 26) and full-time students (under age 32) with plane tickets and anyone who wants

Trans-Siberian tickets (tel. 974-1781 or 974-1798, fax 280-7686, e-mail: star@glas.apc.org).

Eating in Moscow

Many of Moscow's restaurants are expensive, but reasonable places exist and Russian fast food-places are popping up.

Moscow's a good place to try Georgian cuisine. It's an easy choice for vegetarians. **Restoran Mziuri** is more convenient (daily 12:00–24:00, in the basement of the Georgian Cultural Center at Arbat 42) and **Guria** (Гурия) is more popular (Komsomolskii/Комсомольский prospekt 7/3, in the courtyard near the corner of ulitsa Timura Frunze, Metro: Park Kultury/Парк Културы). In both cases it is advisable to go only for lunch when reservations are unnecessary. At neither should a full meal cost you more than $15.

The secret to ordering Georgian food is appetizers. A nice Georgian meal for three or four might consist of one each of the following: *khachapuri* (хачапури—dough filled with cheese), a chopped vegetable dish such as *pkhali* (пхали—chopped cabbage), chicken *satsivi* (сациви—diced chicken in a spicy yellow sauce), *baklazhan* (баклажан—eggplant), *lobio* (Лобио—a bean dish served either hot or cold), and plenty of *lavash* (лаваш—bread). If you want soup, try *kharcho* (харчо), a spicy broth with lots of meat and onions. Main dishes are less special, usually just some kind of grilled or skewered meat. Tell them you don't eat meat, order two or three appetizers per person, and you'll cut down the size of the bill and still get the best dishes.

Russkii Bistro, one of about 20 newly opened "Russian kitchens," serves Russian fast food: meat and vegetable pies, various main meals, tasty pastries, and intriguing beverages. Try *kvas* (a refreshing drink made from bread) or *medovoucha* (a fermented mead-like drink). No English spoken, but pointing is welcomed (Monday–Saturday 9:00–23:00, Sunday from 10:00, Tverskaya 19, next to the Pushkinskaya McDonald's).

Kombi's (Комби'с) is Moscow's closest thing to a Western sub shop, selling sandwiches for $3 to $5 and their trademark Oreo milkshakes for $1.75. They have an English menu. There are several locations in Moscow, all open daily from 10:00 to 22:00. One is very near Red Square at ulitsa Tverskaya/ Тверская 4, across the street from the Hotel Intourist near Metro: Okhotnii Ryad/Охотный Ряд; another is at ulitsa

Tverskaya 32, across the street from the exit of Metro: Mayakovskaya/Маяковская (go left at the top of the escalators); another is at Arbat 40.

Patio Pizza (Патио Пицца) is a large pizza, pasta, and salad restaurant with trademark red-and-white-checked tablecloths and glassed-in terraces. It seems more a part of American suburbia than of Moscow. A good all-you-can-eat salad bar costs $8; whole pizzas start at $7; spaghetti and meatballs are $8; lasagna, tortellini, or Russian *permini* cost $11; and credit cards are accepted. One location is at ulitsa Volkhonka/Волхонка 13a, across the street from the Pushkin Museum; you can walk from the Kremlin, or take the Metro to Kropotkinskaya/Кропоткинская (go out the exit toward the center). The other Patio Pizza is in the terrace underneath the Hotel Intourist on ulitsa Tverskaya/Тверская. (Both are open daily 12:00–24:00.)

Near the **Mayakovskaya**/Маяковская Metro station at the top end of ulitsa Tverskaya/Тверская is a potpourri of good restaurants. **Patio Pasta**, related to Patio Pizza, is on the northwest corner of the square and serves up pasta dishes for $7 to $12 (daily 12:00–24:00, 1st Tverskaya-Yamskaya/1я Тверская-Ямская ulitsa 1). **Tandoor,** an Indian restaurant with vegetable entrees for $8 to $11, meat entrees for $14 to $19, and rice for $3, is on the southeast corner of the square (daily 12:00–23:00, ulitsa Tverskaya 30). Across the street is the **American Bar & Grill** (Американский Бар & Гриль,), with salads and burgers from $6, and burritos for $10, as well as breakfast (open 24 hours, ulitsa Tverskaya 32). Next door is **Kombi's** (see above). For Kombi's, the American Bar & Grill, and Tandoor, go left at the top of the escalators if you're coming from the Metro.

Inside **GUM** are a few quick stand-up and fast-food restaurants, not worth a special trip but fine for sightseers who need a midday sandwich. For example **Rostik's** (Ростик'с), on the second floor of GUM in the northeast corner, is a fast-food chicken restaurant where it costs $5 to gnaw on two pieces of roast chicken and a roll (daily 10:00–20:00; use the separate entrance on Sunday).

McDonald's (МакДоналдс) golden arches attract Muscovites and foreigners alike with cleanliness, efficiency, relatively cheap prices, and predictably edible food. Moscow's oldest and biggest is at Metro: Pushkinskaya/Пушкинская, directly across from the statue of Russia's beloved national poet, Aleksandr Pushkin. In the tradition of Soviet gigantism and American capitalism, Mickey D's boasts 27 cash registers, 1,500 employees with beaming smiles, seating for over 700, and nearly 40,000 customers a day (daily 8:00–24:00).

Farmer's market: Central Moscow's largest and best market is the Danilovskii Rynok (Даниловский Рынок). Take the Metro one stop south of the Ring on the gray line to Tulskaya/Тульская. Exit toward the center and make your way across the busy intersection to the large circular building with the white, dome-like top.

Grocery stores: These are proliferating in Moscow, and it is no longer necessary to trek halfway across the city to find a decent selection of groceries. One of the best supermarkets in Moscow—although it still uses the three-line system—is the **Torgovi Dom Novoarbatskii** at Novii Arbat/Новыи Арбат. From Metro: Arbatskaya/Арбатская, walk about three minutes down Novii Arbat, the street with the monstrous gray Soviet architecture that radiates from the same point as the Arbat pedestrian zone. It's on your left. The downstairs section has a particularly good selection of quality Russian products. Upstairs is a separate open-shelf section with imported goods only (Monday–Saturday 8:00–22:00, Sunday 9:00–21:00).

Transportation Connections—Moscow

By Train

Foreigners in Moscow normally buy train tickets at one of the four offices of the Moscow Central Railway Agency. You can

Station Guide

Trains to:	Leave from:	Nearest Metro:
Warsaw and Vilnius	Belorusskii Vokzal	Belorusskaya/ Белорусская
Riga	Rizhskii Vokzal	Rizhskaya/Рижская
Tallinn and St. Petersburg	Leningradskii Vokzal	Komsomolskaya/ Комсомолская

Trains Departing Moscow

#	To	Leaves	Arrives	2nd class	1st class
1	Riga (Рига)	20:00	10:30	$54	$107
3	"	21:16	12:25	"	"
34	Tallinn (Таллинн)	18:30	9:00	$62	$103
5	Vilnius (Вильнюс)	17:17	10:23	$48	$86
9	Warsaw (Варшава)	15:35	9:43	$68	$110
32	Helsinki (Хельсинки)	22:17	11:30	$93	$160
24	St. Petersburg				
	(Санкт-Петербург)	12:24	20:15	$37-$47*	$78
12	"	12:27	20:50	"	"
160	"	17:20	23:11	"	"
14	"	20:35	4:35	"	"
28	"	21:30	5:40	"	"
10	"	22:50	6:40	"	"
26	"	23:00	7:10	"	"
6		23:10	7:35	"	"
2	"	23:55	8:25	"	"
4	"	23:59	8:29	"	"
20	"	1:00	10:07	"	"
30	"	1:52	11:00	"	"

Prices vary according to train, speed, and day of the week. Generally, the lower the number, the more expensive (and nicer) the train.

visit whichever office is most convenient; I prefer the Krasnoprudnaya ulitsa office at Metro: Komsomolskaya. The following offices are open daily 8:00 to 13:00 and 14:00 to 19:00.

Moscow's Railway Offices

Krasnoprudnaya/Краснопрудная ulitsa 1, on the first floor of the brown nine-floor apartment building next to Yaroslavskii Vokzal at Metro: Komsomolskaya/Комсомольская. It says Центральное Железнодорожное Агенство in green letters over the door. Windows 10 and 11 are for foreigners buying tickets to destinations within the ex–Soviet Union. Windows 4 through 7 are for tickets to foreign countries such as Poland and Finland. Window 3 is for information, and window 2 is the *administrator* (the office boss).

Leningradskii/Ленинградский prospekt 1, behind Belorusskii Vokzal (station). Metro: Belorusskaya/Белорусская. You can reach it by crossing the bridge across the tracks to the yellow-and-white building; go in the farthest entrance.

Mozhaiskii/Можайский Val 4/6, near Metro: Kievskaya/Киевская.

Malii Kharitonevskii/Малый Харитоньевский pereulok 6/11 (the head, but least convenient, office). From Metro: Turgenevskaya/Тургеневская, go northeast on ulitsa Myasnitskaya/Мясницкая; take second right on Malii Kharitonevskii.

Foreigners are usually not permitted to buy tickets from the regular windows at the stations that most Russians use, and foreigners pay a higher price for train tickets than do Russians. Bring your passport, visa, or some other form of ID when you buy tickets so that the clerks can copy your name onto your ticket. It's usually possible to get round-trip tickets to St. Petersburg, but you can't count on it.

Train Ticket Exceptions

Another way to get Tallinn or St. Petersburg tickets: The Intourist windows 19 and 20 (24 hours daily, on the second floor of Leningradskii Vokzal at Metro: Komsomolskaya/Комсомольская) sell tickets to Tallinn and St. Petersburg for trains leaving *the same day or the next day only*. Their prices are slightly higher than at the Central Railway Agency. Go in the main hall of the station, up the stairs in the far right corner of the hall, through the door on your right, and then to the left.

Same-day or next-day tickets to Helsinki: These are available *only* at windows 33 through 36 in a small special office on the second floor of Leningradskii Vokzal, on the left as you walk into the station's main hall (daily 8:00–13:00, 14:00–20:00). It's slightly cheaper to go by train to St. Petersburg and then on to Helsinki. If you must take the train direct to Helsinki, it's more convenient to buy tickets in advance from one of the four Central Railway Agency offices.

By Air

Connections between the Airport and Downtown: A taxi to or from Moscow's Sheremetyevo-2 Airport will run you at least $30 and possibly $50. If you can carry your luggage, the alternative is a bus-Metro combination which costs pennies. Bus #551, and a faster "Express" bus on the same route, run between Sheremetyevo and Metro: Rechnoi Vokzal/Речной Вокзал, the northern terminus of the green Metro line. The Express bus fare is just under $1, and bus #551 just requires Moscow bus tickets. The bus stop at Sheremetyevo-2 is a short walk out from the terminal, near the parking lot, past the taxi-Mafia gauntlet. The trip to Rechnoi Vokzal can take up to 45 minutes, a half-hour if you catch the express. Allow at least another 45 minutes on the Metro. These buses also service the domestic Sheremetyevo-1 terminal on the other side of the runways; don't get off here.

For booking and reconfirmation: British Airways, Krasnopresnenskaya naberezhnaya 12, #1905, use entrance #3, tel. 258-2492; Delta, Krasnopresnenskaya naberezhnaya 12 #1102a, use entrance #3, tel. 258-1288; Finnair, Kuznetskii Most 3, tel. 292-1758; LOT, Korovii val 7, tel. 238-0003 or 238-0313; Lufthansa, Olymic Penta Hotel, Olympiiskii Prospekt 18/1, tel. 975-2501; Malev, Povarskaya 21, tel. 202-8416; SAS, Kuznetskii Most 3, tel. 925-4747.

ST. PETERSBURG

Once a swamp, then an imperial capital, and now a showpiece of vanished aristocratic opulence shot through with the grimy ruins of socialism, St. Petersburg is Russia's most accessible and most tourist-worthy city. Standing in Palace Square, you'll shiver and think, "The revolution started here." (You may also shiver and think, "I'm as far north as Alaska.") Palaces, gardens, statues, and arched bridges over graceful canals bring back the time of the czars. Two of the world's greatest art museums top it off. Amid such artistic and historical splendor, modern Russia and its problems seem terribly out of place, but here they are: streets of legless beggars, Mafia-controlled kiosks, wheezing buses, shabby bread stores, broken signs, exhaust-stained facades, pornography dealers, and ice-cream stands in see-your-breath weather.

Compared to Moscow, St. Petersburg is compact, walkable, friendly, manageable, and architecturally intact. Don't get overly uptight about timing your visit to the summer solstice for St. Petersburg's much-bandied "White Nights." You'll be able to enjoy bright evenings here all summer long. If you want the real midnight sun, go to Finland.

Save a sunny day just to walk. Keep your head up—ugly Soviet shops mar the first floor of many buildings, but the upper facades are sun-warmed and untouched by street grime. Make sure you get off Nevsky Prospekt to explore the back streets along the canals. Climb St. Isaac's Cathedral for the view. Visit the Summer Gardens. The next day, when the

St. Petersburg

Baltic Sea brings clouds and drizzle, plunge into the Hermitage or the Russian Museum.

Planning Your Time

Day 1: 10:00, after breakfast, take a leisurely walk along Nevsky Prospekt to acquaint yourself with the city; 11:00, climb up St. Isaac's Cathedral; 11:30, walk back to Sadko's for lunch; 13:30, the Russian Museum is just up the street; 18:30, taxi to the Korean House for dinner.

Day 2: 10:30, tour the Hermitage; 13:30, have lunch at the Count Suvorov or Bistro Laima; 15:00, take the Metro to the Peter and Paul Fortress; 18:30, come back to the center for dinner at Tandoor.

Day 3 (optional): Spend more time in the Hermitage, visit the Piskaryovskoe cemetery, or go to Petrodvorets for the day.

Orientation

Get to know Nevsky Prospekt (Невский Проспект), St. Petersburg's main street. Almost everything you'll want to see is either along Nevsky or between it and the river. A few spots, like the Finland train station and the Peter and Paul Fortress, are just across the river.

Nevsky starts at the slender-spired Admiralty, next to the river and the Winter Palace. Running outward from the city it crosses three canals: first the Moika (Мойка), then Kanal Griboyedova (Канал Грибоедова), and finally the Fontanka (Фонтанка). Tourist Nevsky ends a little farther out at Ploshchad Vosstaniya (Uprising Square, Площадь Восстания), home to a tall obelisk and the Moskovskii train station.

Walking distances are manageable (from Ploshchad Vosstaniya to the Admiralty takes 30–45 minutes), and St. Petersburg has enough natural landmarks that on a nice summer day you can easily get around on foot without using a map.

Tourist Information: Ost-West Kontact Service, a private information office run by Westerners, is the closest thing to a tourist information office that St. Pete has to offer (Monday–Saturday 10:00–18:00, Sunday 12:00–18:00, ul. Mayakovskogo 7, down the road from the Nevsky Palace Hotel, tel. 279-7045, fax 327-3417, mailing address P.O. Box 109, SF-53101 Lappeenranta, Finland). They give out tourist info and book theater tickets, cruises, bus tours, homestays, and hotel rooms. If you arrange accommodations in advance with Ost-West, they will send you a visa support letter, and if you want to visit Russian friends in St. Petersburg they will set up the invitation for $7 per night, which is much less bother than having your friends work through OVIR.

English-language periodicals like *Pulse* and the *St. Petersburg Times,* which comes out on Tuesday and Friday, will keep you up to date on events in the city.

American Embassy: Furshtadtskaya/Фурштадтская ulitsa 15, Metro: Chernyshevskaya/Чернышевская, tel. 275-1701.

Bookstore: The **Mir** (Мир) international bookshop at Nevsky Prospekt 13, near Palace Square, has lots of new and used art books, English fiction (in the back room), and St.

Petersburg maps at better prices than the outdoor stalls (daily 10:00–14:00 and 15:00–19:00).

Guides: Local guides are cheap, eager, and helpful. Try Alexandra Ivanova (who gives Hermitage tours, gets cheap tickets for concerts and ballets, and even takes people to the airport, $20/hr, tel. 232-6458), and Alexy Alyoshetkin (who tailors sightseeing to your needs, $5/hr for city walking tours, $20/day for 2–3 days, tel. 543-8475).

Currency Exchange
6,000 rubles = about $1

It's available everywhere and ATMs are increasingly common. Exchange offices are usually closed by 18:00 weekday evenings and all day on weekends. The American Express office is inside the Grand Hotel Europe (Monday–Friday 9:00–17:00, Saturday 9:00–13:00, Mikhailovskaya/Михайловская ulitsa 1, Metro: Nevsky Prospekt/Невский Проспект, tel. 329-6060). Their exchange desk is run by a Russian bank, not by Amex; at last report they took a 1 percent commission on traveler's checks. Emergency check cashing is available, but not cash advances.

Telephones and Mail

Brand-new, bright green card telephones have sprouted along the streets of St. Petersburg. Cards are available at shops and offices throughout the city—for example, at Ost-West Kontact Service. The cheapest card costs about $9 for 100 units. For each minute, local calls cost 1 unit; to Moscow or the Baltics, 14 units; to Europe, 22; and to America, 54. The older public phones use the same tokens as the Metro.

You can also make long-distance calls at the central telephone office at Bolshaya Morskaya/Большая Морская ulitsa 5 (between Palace Square and Nevsky Prospekt on the street with the big arches; look for the "PHONE" sign). For calls within the former Soviet Union, enter and turn right to Hall #1; a booth sells wide-grooved tokens for the intercity phones in the surrounding booths numbered 15 through 37 (24 hours daily). One 40-cent token buys 43 seconds to Moscow. For international calls, go to Halls #2 and #3. In Hall #2, you pick up a numbered token, go to the cabin with that number, make your call, and pay afterwards (daily 8:00–23:00). Or if you choose, Hall #3 provides operator assistance: fill out a form and wait to

St. Petersburg Metro

ПЕТРОГРАДСКАЯ (PETROGRADSKAYA)

ГОРЬКОВСКАЯ (GORKOVSKAYA)

NEVA RIVER

ПЛ. ЛЕНИНА (PL. LENINA)

NOT TO SCALE — TRANSFER STATIONS

ПРИМОРСКАЯ (PRIMORSKAYA)

ГОСТИНЫЙ ДВОР (GOSTINII DVOR)

ЧЕРНЫШЕВСКАЯ (CHERNYSHEVSKAYA)

ВАСИЛЕОСТРОВСКАЯ (VASILEOSTROVSKAYA)

МАЯКОВСКАЯ (MAYAKOVSKAYA)

ПЛ. ВОССТАНИЯ (PL. VOSSTANIYA)

НЕВСКИЙ ПРОСПЕКТ (NEVSKY PROSPECT)

ДОСТОЕВСКАЯ (DOSTOEVSKAYA)

НОВОЧЕРКАССКАЯ (NOVOCHERKASSKAYA)

СЕННАЯ (SENNAYA)

САДОВАЯ (SADOVAYA)

ВЛАДИМИРСКАЯ (VLADIMIRSKAYA)

ПЛ. АЛЕКСАНДРА НЕВСКОГО (PL. ALEXANDRA NEVSKOGO)

ТЕХНОЛОГИЧЕСКИЙ ИНСТИТУТ (TECHNOLOGICHESKY INSTITUT)

ЛИГОВСКИЙ ПРОСПЕКТ (LIGOVSKY PROSPECT)

ВАЛТИЙСКАЯ (BALTIISKAYA)

TO МОСКОВСКАЯ (MOSKOVSKAYA) + AIRPORT BUSES

НАРВСКАЯ (NARVSKAYA)

— ESSENTIAL METRO WORDS —
- ENTRANCE – ВХОД
- EXIT (TO CITY) – ВЫХОД (В ГОРОД)
- TRANSFER – ПЕРЕХОД
- WHERE IS... – ГДЕ...

be told when your party answers; you're liable for one minute if an answering machine responds (24 hours daily). Calls to America or Europe cost about $2.60 per minute (cheaper after 20:00 and on weekends). On most phones at this office you have to push the "Ответ" button when the other side answers. Hall #4 is all new with the cheapest photocopies, computer rentals, e-mail, and fax services in town (daily 9:00–21:00), along with comfortable card-operated phone booths and a DHL express mail office.

The central post office is at Pochtamtskaya/Почтамтская ulitsa 9, under the arch a couple of blocks down from St. Isaac's Cathedral. Send international mail from window 24 (Monday–Saturday 9:00–19:30, Sunday 10:00–17:45).

Getting Around St. Petersburg

The Metro is not that helpful for getting around the center of the city, but essential for longer trips. It requires metal tokens which you can buy at station entrances for 30 cents and which also work in the pay phones. Trams and buses can be quite useful, but it takes some time to familiarize yourself with stops and routes. Buy yourself a street map. The Mir bookstore at

Nevsky 13 has the best selection, but you can also try the Dom Knigi bookstore at Nevsky 28, or street stalls.

Taxis are a good option in St. Petersburg. You should pay the ruble equivalent of about $2 for an average trip within the center. Pay $1 if it's just a hop, skip, and a jump. Longer trips will run $3 to $5. Some cabs are official and use the meter. Unofficial cab drivers around major tourist sights may try to rip you off; refuse any driver who asks for payment in dollars.

Sights—Along Nevsky Prospekt

▲▲▲**Hermitage** (Эрмитаж)—The Hermitage's vast collection of European masters makes it one of the world's top art museums, ranking up there with the Louvre and the Prado. Some people come to Russia just to see this place. Others don't want to spend time on painters whose work can be admired more easily in New York, Paris, or Madrid. The first sort of person could spend days inside without exhausting the Hermitage's treasures; the second might want to bypass the place entirely in favor of the Russian Museum (see below) or no museums at all.

Here's a middle strategy. First, pick *one* artistic period that you really like, and head straight for that. Modern art is on the top floor, antiquities at ground level, and everything in between on the second floor.

Second, visit rooms 188 through 198 on the second floor, where the attraction is history, not art. Russian royalty once partied and feasted in these begilded, bedraped, and bejeweled chambers. In 1917, the Provisional Government met for the very last time in the green-pillared Malachite Hall (room 198), before being arrested in the adjacent dining room. The building faces Palace Square, where Bolshevik forces assembled before storming in.

The museum is in the czars' old Winter Palace, the green-and-white building between Palace Square and the river. The museum entrance is on the other, riverfront side of the building ($10, free for students with ISIC cards, Tuesday–Sunday 10:30–18:00, closed Monday, ticket windows close an hour before the museum, top floor closes 40 minutes early).

The number of people employed at the Hermitage is amazing—practically each one of the hundreds of rooms has an attendant.

Nevsky Prospekt

▲▲**Russian Museum** (Русский Музей)—Here's a fascinating collection of prerevolutionary Russian art, particularly 18th- and 19th-century painting and portraiture. People who complain that the Hermitage is just more Monets and Rembrandts love the Russian Museum, since the artists are less well-known in the West. Much of the work reveals Russians exploring their own landscape: marshes, birch stands, muddy village streets, the conquest of Siberia, and firelit scenes in family huts. You'll see Repin's portrait of Tolstoy standing barefoot in the woods. You may enjoy Rerikh, an early 20th-century Russian artist who painted startling, imaginary, Himalayan landscapes in icy blue colors, or Vrubel's painting of *The Russian Hero*. Use either the main entrance, closer to the medieval art, or the side door along Kanal Griboyedova, closer to the early 20th-century paintings ($8, students $4, guided tours $20, free the first Wednesday of every month; Wednesday–Monday 10:00–18:00, closed Tuesday; ticket window closes an hour before the museum; Inzhenernaya/ Инженерная ulitsa 4, a block off Nevsky behind the Grand Hotel Europe).

▲▲▲**Churches**—Russian Orthodox churches are reopening all over St. Petersburg and Moscow. When you see onion domes, walk in. Smaller churches are full of Russians morning, noon, and night, and will give you more of a feeling for Russian religion than will church-museums like St. Isaac's or the Kazan Cathedral. Plus, entrance is usually free, though you can leave a small donation toward renovation, or buy and light a candle. In St. Petersburg, drop by the Church of Our Savior for its fabulous mozaics ($2.50, Thursday–Tuesday 11:00–19:00, closed Wednesday)—it's the interesting domed church near the Russian Museum. There's also a nice church at Vladimirskaya/ Владимирская Metro, across from the indoor market, and another at the south end of Mokhovaya/ Моховая ulitsa, by the first bridge across the Fontanka going north from Nevsky. For the best Orthodox service in St. Petersburg, take the Metro to ploshchad Aleksandra Nevskovo (Пл. Александра Невского) and attend the church in the *lavra* (seminary) across the street from the Metro exit, either on Sunday morning or for evening services daily at 18:00. It doesn't cost anything, unless you want to see Dostoevsky's grave in the cemetery across from the lavra (entrance $1).

▲▲**St. Isaac's Cathedral** (Исаакиевский Собор)—Head down Malaya Morskaya/Малая Морская ulitsa from Nevsky Prospekt. Your mission, should you decide to accept it, is to climb the colonnade stairway to the roof. The view is worth the climb and the money. Russians buy tickets at the booth outside the fence; foreigners have to go to the desk just inside the door. The inside of St. Isaac's is a museum, not a functioning church, and at $8 for the museum, $3 for the colonnade (students $4 and $1), I'd recommend simply taking a peek at the massive 19th-century interior while you buy your cheaper colonnade ticket. You can (and should) visit a real Russian house of worship for nothing (Thursday–Tuesday 11:00–18:00, last entry at 17:00, closed Wednesday).

▲**Kazan Cathedral** (Казанский Собор)—Reopened after years as a Museum of Atheism, this huge brown cathedral is on Nevsky at Kanal Griboyedova. It's not quite yet a functioning church either, but entrance is free (daily 9:00–18:00); one wing houses a museum of the history of religion ($3, students $1.50, Thursday–Tuesday 11:00–17:00, closed Wednesday).

▲▲**Nevsky Prospekt itself**—Nevsky's architectural highlights include the magnificent arch of the General Staff Building down Bolshaya Morskaya ulitsa, the Kazan Cathedral, and the views down the canals. You should also check out the sign at Nevsky 14, preserved from World War II, warning citizens that the north side of the street was more dangerous during shelling. The building with the distinctive tower at #28 is the city's main Dom Knigi bookstore, formerly the Russian headquarters of the Singer sewing machine company.

▲**Boat trips**—From June into September, trips on the St. Petersburg canals leave every half-hour from a dock on the Fontanka at Nevsky Prospekt (about $6).

▲**Dostoevski Museum** (Музей Ф. М. Достоевского)—Although much of the furnishings are gone, you can get some feel for how the famous writer lived from visiting the six-room apartment where he wrote *The Brothers Karamazov*. Duck when you enter. Captions are in English. The *babushki* who run the place put a new half-cup of tea on Dostoevski's desk every morning ($2.50, students $1.25, Tuesday–Sunday 11:00–18:30, last entry 17:30, closed Monday and the last Wednesday of every month; Kuznechii/Кузнечый pereulok 5, a block from Metro: Dostoevskaya/Достоевская).

Sights—Across the River

The first two sights, the Fortress and Kunstkamera, are within walking distance of the Hermitage.

▲**Peter and Paul Fortress** (Петропавловская Крепость)—Founded by Peter the Great in 1703 during the Great Northern War with Sweden, this fortress on an island in the Neva was the birthplace of the city of St. Petersburg. Its gold steeple catches the sunlight, and the blank walls face the Winter Palace across the river. You can wander through and climb the bastions for free. Your ticket lets you into the church (where Peter is buried), the jail (which housed numerous 19th-century revolutionaries including Lenin's older brother), and several museum-style exhibits. The main entrance is through the park from Metro: Gorkovskaya/ Горьковская. Buy tickets inside the museum gift shop opposite the church, or from the "касса" to your right after you cross the bridge onto the island ($3, students half-price, Thursday–Monday 11:00–18:00, Tuesday 11:00–17:00, ticket office closes one hour earlier; fortress closed Wednesday and the last Tuesday of each month).

Moored in the river along Petrogradskaya nab. not far from the fortress is the Cruiser *Aurora* (Крейсер "Аврора"), which fired the shot that signaled the start of the Russian Revolution. Now a museum, it's worth visiting if you are a history buff or a Bolshevik, and with the Lenin Museum in Moscow closed, the *Aurora* now has one of Russia's best collections of Soviet kitsch (free, Tuesday–Thursday and Saturday–Sunday 10:30–16:00, no English descriptions).

Halfway between the Peter and Paul Fortress and the *Aurora*, at Petrovskaya nab. 6, is Peter the Great's log cabin, entombed in a small 19th-century brick house in a tiny park. Peter lived here briefly in 1703.

▲**Kunstkamera** (Кунсткамера)—This is officially known as the Peter the Great Museum of Anthropology and Ethnography. Truthfully, though, most people come only for the collection of hideously deformed preserved fetuses that Peter the Great bought from an Amsterdam doctor and had brought back to Russia. The rest is a vast, dusty, poorly lit collection of Soviet-era dioramas and displays on world cultures. Check out the excellent American Indian section, the "Our Baltic Neighbors" display, or the selection of photographs of socialist Africa's public buildings. No English captions. ($2, Friday–Wednesday 11:00–18:00, entrance until 16:45, closed Thursday, Universitetskaya naberezhnaya 3, in the blue-and-white building across the big bridge from the Hermitage.)

▲**Piskaryovskoe Memorial Cemetery** (Пискарёвское Мемориальное Кладбище)—This is a memorial to the hundreds of thousands who died in the city during the German siege of Leningrad in World War II. The cemetery, with its eternal flame, acres of mass grave bunkers (marked only with the year of death), moving statue of Mother Russia, and many pilgrims bringing flowers to remember lost loved ones, is an awe-inspiring experience even for an American tourist to whom the siege of Leningrad is just another page from the history books. To reach the cemetery, take the Metro north to Ploshchad Muzhestva (Площадь Мужества), exit, walk through the large brick apartment complex to the street, cross it to the eastbound bus stop, and take bus #123 to the sixth stop—you'll see the buildings on your left.

Day Trip from St. Petersburg

▲▲**Peterhof** (Петергоф)—If you have time for a short day trip, go to Peter the Great's lavish palace at Peterhof, also known as Petrodvorets (Петродворец), along the Gulf of Finland west of the city. This is Russia's Versailles and the target of many tour groups and travel poster photographers. Promenade along the grand canal, which runs through landscaped grounds from the boat dock up to the terraced fountains in front of the palace. There are ice-cream stands aplenty and a nice indoor café with coffee and pastries. You can visit the museum inside the palace for $3, but it's more fun to stay outdoors. Children love to run past the so-called trick fountains—sometimes they splash you, sometimes they don't. In summer, "Meteor" hydrofoils leave for Peterhof every half-hour during the daytime from a dock across from the Hermitage entrance (30-minute trip, $8 each way, plus $6 entry to the palace grounds). In winter, you have to take a suburban train and then switch to a bus—ask for details (Tuesday–Sunday 11:00–8:00, closed Monday and last Tuesday of month; even when palace is closed, fountains still run).

Ballet, Opera, and Music

Keep an eye out for ballet and opera performances, advertised on posters all around town. The Marinskii (formerly Kirov)

Ballet performs in Teatralnaya Ploshchad (Театральная Площадь), a little ways southwest of Nevsky—you may need to take a taxi. More convenient is the Malii Opera (Театр оперы и балета), which also has ballet, at ploshchad Isskustv/ Исскуств 1, by the Russian Museum. The symphony is on Mikhailovskaya/Михайловская ulitsa across the street from the Grand Hotel Europe; the box office is next door. The theaters in St. Petersburg have cleaned up their act and scalpers have become extinct. Just go to the box office for tickets (usually open daily 11:00–19:00; closed for a lunch break at 14:00 or 15:00). The most popular ballets sell out a few days in advance, but for others there are seats left the day of the performance. At the Malii, foreigners pay about $25 for the nicest seats, less than $5 in the upper balconies. Symphony tickets are always cheaper. If you don't want to brave the box office, your hostel, hotel, or Ost-West may be able to help you with tickets.

Sleeping in St. Petersburg
(If calling from the U.S.A., dial 011-7-812, then the local number; for more phone info, see the Appendix: Dialing Direct Within Russia & the Baltics.)

Hostels
St. Petersburg International Hostel is a normal hostel like those in Western Europe, with friendly English-speaking staff, 60 beds in clean three- to five-bed rooms with clean showers, hot water year-round, a skimpy kitchen (BYO pot), a small shop, a cybercafé for Internet addicts, and Western movies every night. Nineteen dollars a night (hostel members $17) includes a continental breakfast (credit cards accepted). They're busy in summer, so reserve ahead by phone (tel. 329-8018, fax 329-8019, Web site: www.spb.su/ryh, e-mail: ryh@ryh.spb.su). Their mailing address is P.O. Box 8, SF-53501 Lappeenranta, Finland, but it's faster to contact them by fax, phone, or e-mail. You can also book through the Hostelling International booking network (tel. 202/783-6161 in the U.S.A.; expect to be on hold a long time, ask for Customer Service) or Helsinki's Eurohostel (Linnankatu 9, 00160 Helsinki, tel. 09/622-0470, fax 09/655-044, Web site: www. eurohostel.fi). If the hostel is full, St. Pete's will confirm you for Holiday Hostel (below).

The best thing about the St. Petersburg International Hostel is its efficient system of visa support. It will save time if your first communication includes your full legal name; citizenship; birthdate; passport number and expiration date; dates you plan to stay at the hostel; place, date, and means of entry into Russia; place, date, and means of exit from Russia; location of the Russian consulate where you plan to have your visa processed; Visa or MasterCard number; your name as it is written on the credit card; card expiration date; and signature. They need this information to make up your visa support letter and confirmation voucher. Remember to include your fax number so they can respond. The hostel will charge you $54 ($25 for visa support, $10 fax fee, and $19 for your first night's stay at the hostel).

Once you send all your details to the hostel, they will send you a confirmation voucher and your visa support letter, which you can take or send to the nearest Russian consulate or embassy to get your visa. Ask and you will usually receive visa support for several days longer than you plan to stay in the hostel, which gives you the flexibility to stay longer without ridiculous extension hassles.

The hostel will also take reservations ($10 fee) for Holiday Hostel in St. Petersburg, Travellers Guest House and Heritage Hostel in Moscow, and for the new hostel in Irkutsk. They'll provide visa support for these stays, and can arrange transportation to the airport or train station.

At 3rd Sovetskaya/3я Советская ulitsa 28, the hostel is about a ten-minute walk from Nevsky Prospekt, Ploshchad Vosstaniya, the Moskovskii Vokzal (train station), and the associated Metro stations. Coming out the front door of the train station, walk right, heading into the major street with overhead trolley wires. Take your first left off this street onto Suvorovskii/Суворовский prospekt. Walk 2 blocks (past the blue signs of the Philips housewares store) and then turn right onto 3rd Sovetskaya ulitsa. The hostel is the remodeled cream-and-magenta building half a block down on your left.

Downstairs you'll see Sindbad Travel, a fully accredited budget and student travel agency like STA and Council Travel in the U.S.A. Run by the hostel, Sindbad sells train and air tickets at fair prices (Monday–Friday 9:30–17:30, tel. 327-8384, fax 329-8019, e-mail: sindbad@ryh.spb.su).

Holiday Hostel has more doubles and more congenial

common space, and has a nicer view than the International Hostel. On the other hand, the bathrooms are not as modern, the door is harder to find and get into, the hostel is not as tightly run, and it is beyond walking distance from Nevsky Prospekt (ulitsa Mikhailova/Михайлова, tel. 542-7364 or 327-1070, fax 325-8559, Web site: www.spb.su/holiday, e-mail: postmaster@hostelling.spb.su). Holiday Hostel has about 100 beds in two- to six-bed rooms on several floors of a larger building, charges $18 to $22 per person per night (depending on the season), and can provide visa support by fax. Breakfast is included and laundry service is available. Visa and Master-Card accepted.

The hostel is less than a five-minute walk from the Ploshchad Lenina (Площадь Ленина) Metro station at the Finlyandskii Vokzal (train station). Coming out the front door of the Metro station, walk straight down through the park to the river, then turn left 1 block to ulitsa Mikhailova; the hostel is in the building on the far left corner with the fourth-floor corner balcony. The hostel entrance is in the inside corner of the L-shaped building; go in through the archway off of ulitsa Mikhailova, look for the "YH" sign on the wall, and ring the bell—the hostel is on the first floor. (You can't get in by yourself without punching in the code they'll give you.)

Homestays

Host Family Association sets up homestays with families in St. Petersburg for $30 for one person, $50 for two, or $60 single/$90 double with all the meals. Contact them by e-mail at alexei@hofak.hop.stu.neva.ru, or use tel. & fax 7/812/275-1992 (St. Petersburg office). Along with providing visa support, they'll meet you at the train (for $12) or the airport (for $30) and bring you to your hosts' apartment.

White Nights arranges homestays ($25/night with breakfast) and hotels ($50–100 per room with breakfast) in St. Petersburg and Moscow, and provides visa support. They also specialize in kayak trips, Russian language classes, Trans-Siberian train tickets, and getting travelers way out in the Russian toolies. Ideally, contact their Russian office via e-mail (Web site: www.concourse.net/bus/wnights/, e-mail: wnights@russia.spb.su), but if you lack e-mail, contact the Sacramento office at tel. & fax 916/979-9381).

Hotels

The St. Petersburg hotel scene is frustrating. The cheaper hotels—with doubles under $50—are usually too sleazy or too far from the Metro. Hotels with new furniture, appealing bathrooms, and a modern lobby start at $100 for a double, and even that often means a pompous Soviet-style reception desk, congealed breakfast, distant location, shady characters in the lobby, and $40,000 cars (without license plates) parked outside. What's more, these hotels generally aren't together enough to fax you an invitation letter to support your visa application. For enlightened service, propriety, and visa support in the center of the city, there are first-world fortresses such as the Nevsky Palace (tel. 275-2001), the Grand Hotel Europe (tel. 329-6000), and the Astoria (tel. 210-5757), but they cost upwards of $200 a night. Here are a few places worth recommending:

The cheapest of the high-price hotels (though its rooms are correspondingly small—it's a ship, after all) is the Swiss-run **Hotelship Peterhof,** moored at naberezhnaya Makarova 24 (tel. 325-8888, fax 325-8889), where double rooms start at $190 (reserve at 415/398-7947 in the U.S.A.).

Hotel Deson-Ladoga (Десон-Ладога) is a safe bet. The rooms are nice, the reception staff speaks English, and it's only a block from the Novocherkasskaya metro. If you book your room through Ost-West Kontact Service or through a tour operator, you'll pay less than $100 for a double; otherwise you'll pay $120 for a double or $105 for a single (skip the hotel's restaurant, Prospekt Shaumyana/Шаумяна 26, 195213 St. Petersburg, tel. 528-5200, fax 528-5448).

If you're already in Russia, don't need visa support, and are just looking for a cheap, central, livable hotel with private facilities, try the **Hotel Rus** (Гостиница Русь), on a quiet street just blocks from Nevsky Prospekt (Artilleriiskaya/Артиллерийская ulitsa 1, Metro: Chernyshevskaya/Чернышевская, tel. 273-4683). Built for the 1980 Olympics, it's definitely one of the world's ugliest hotels, but the rooms are standard and the lobby is surprisingly welcoming. Doubles with bath run about $60; the bathrooms are typically Soviet, but OK.

Eating in St. Petersburg

The listings below are your best bets for good food served honestly for $10 to $15 a meal.

At **Koreiskii Domik** (Корейский Домик, i.e., Korean
House), a full meal runs about $12 per person, including tea,
rice, spicy pickled vegetables, and an entreé like *chapche* (noodles with vegetables and meat), *lapsha* (noodles and meat in
broth), or *pulgogi* (spicy Korean-style meat cooked on a burner
on your table). Quick service, English menu. And I've had
their filtered water and never gotten sick. In summer especially, try to reserve at tel. 259-9333 (daily 13:00–22:00). It's at
Izmailovskii/Измайловский prospekt 2, at the intersection with
the Fontanka canal and near the blue-domed church; the
entrance is on Izmailovskii. It's easiest to taxi there along the
Fontanka, but you can get there by foot in 15 to 20 minutes
from Metro: Tekhnologicheskii Institut/Технологический
Институт: walk west on 1я Красноармейская to Izmailovskii,
then take a right to the canal.

Bistro Laima, a "Russian kitchen," serves tasty Russian
fast food such as stroganoff for $4 and fresh o.j. for $2 (sidewalk seating along canal, near side entrance of Russian
Museum and across the canal from Dom Knigi bookstore,
Kanal Griboyedova 16, tel. 315-5545).

Sadko's, the cheapest of the three restaurants in the
Grand Hotel Europe, is St. Petersburg's yuppie American
hangout. Inside it feels like Manhattan. The menu is chalked
on blackboards, and parts of it vary daily. Main dishes cost
about $12 to $18; desserts (great cakes) go for $4 to $8. Beverages are expensive (Cokes, $3.50). There's live music every
evening after about 21:00 or 22:00. Visa, MasterCard, and
Amex accepted. Ask a lady at the bar what her name is, and
she'll answer "$200." (Daily 12:00–01:00, last orders at 00:30,
no nonsmoking section; at the corner of Nevsky Prospekt and
ulitsa Mikhailovskaya/Михайловская, almost across the street
from Gostinii Dvor, tel. 329-6000 for reservations.)

Restaurant Tandoor serves traditional Indian food near
St. Isaac's Cathedral for about $15 per person. The staff speaks
English and accepts credit cards (daily 12:00–23:00, Voznesen-
skii/Вознесенский prospekt 2, at the corner of Admiralteiskii
prospekt, tel. 312-3886).

Count Suvorov (Графъ Суворовъ) is a not-bad place to
get real Russian food for lunch in between a day's sightseeing.
For about $17 you can get, for example, borscht, chicken Kiev,
and your choice of "garnishes" (potato, cauliflower, or French
fries) beautifully presented on big plates in this small, modern

restaurant near the south end of the Gostinii Dvor department store (daily 12:00–24:00, ulitsa Lomonosova/Ломоносова 6, tel. 315-4328).

Kavkaz (Кавказ) is a good Georgian restaurant which you should try if you won't make it to Moscow (see our Georgian food information in the Moscow chapter). A meal in the restaurant will run you $15 to $20. There's also a café (right on the corner of the street) with the same food for much lower prices (e.g., *khachapuri* costs less than a dollar for a quarter-pie). Avoid the "Georgian national soup" (*khashi*). Take the metro to Novocherkasskaya/Новочеркасская, then walk down-hill toward the river and the bridge 1 block; it's on the far right corner (restaurant open daily 12:00–24:00, café open weekdays 10:00–22:00, weekends 10:00–19:00, ulitsa Stakhanovtsev/Стахановцев 5, tel. 221-4309).

In summer the **Afrodite** restaurant runs a beer garden in its courtyard—go through the archway (daily 12:00–01:00, Nevsky 86).

La Cucuracha, a Mexican restaurant staffed by Latin Americans, has $6 enchiladas (Sunday–Thursday 12:00–01:00, Friday–Saturday 12:00–05:00, naberezhnaya Reki Fontanki 39, a block and a half south of Nevsky along the inner side of the Fontanka, tel. 110-4006).

The St. Petersburg **bar scene** centers around Galernaya/Галерная ulitsa, near St. Isaac's. Two popular places are **Senat**, at Galernaya 1, and **Tribunal**, at Senatskaya ploshchad 1.

Picnics

Farmer's market: A trip here will show you the true scope of Russia's agricultural richness (and fill your picnic basket). St. Petersburg's best and most central farmer's market is at Kuznechii/Кузнечый pereulok, right across the street from the Dostoevski museum (look for the big Рынок sign; Metro: Vladimirskaya/Владимирская). Any Russian farmer's market is worth a visit even if you're not shopping. First you'll pass *babushki* selling plastic bags, then Georgians shouting "*Molodoi chelovyek!*" (young man) and "*Devushka!*" (young lady) as they try to entice you toward their piles of oranges, tomatoes, cucumbers, and pears. In the honey (Мёд) section, a chorus line of white-aproned *babushki* stands ready to let you dip and test each kind. Check out the barrels of sauerkraut and trays of pickled garlic and cabbage. In the herbs section, you can sniff massive bunches of fresh coriander (кинза) and wade through a lifetime of horseradish (хрен); nearby, look for a Central Asian spice trader with wares of every color laid out in little bags. (Monday–Saturday 8:00–19:00, Sunday 8:00–16:00, closed one Monday a month for cleaning.)

Grocery stores: There are now small markets in every neighborhood where you can pick up bread, fruit, bottled water, Finnish or Estonian milk, cheese, and yogurt, and other necessities. If you need to do major shopping, the Finnish chain **Stockmann** has a store at Finlyandskii/Финляндский prospekt 1 (daily 10:00–22:00), across the street from the round building of the Hotel St. Petersburg and across the Sampsonievskii Most (bridge) from the Cruiser *Aurora*. This is about three stops on tram #6 from either Metro: Gorkovskaya/Горьковская or Ploshchad Lenina/Площадь Ленина, or you can walk.

Transportation Connections—St. Petersburg

By Train
Stations: Trains to Moscow leave from the Moskovskii Vokzal (Московский Вокзал, Moscow Station, Metro: Ploshchad Vosstaniya/Площадь восстания).

Trains to the Baltics leave from the Varshavskii Vokzal (Варшавский Вокзал, Warsaw Station). Metro: Baltiiskaya/Балтийская brings you to the nearby (and confusingly named) Baltiiskii Vokzal; from the Metro exit, walk to the main street, turn right, and walk 1 long block to the Varshavskii Vokzal.

Trains to Helsinki leave from Finlyandskii Vokzal (Финляндский Вокзал, Finland Station, Metro: Ploshchad Lenina/Площадь Ленина).

Buying Tickets: Tickets for all trains are available without too much hassle at the Central Railway Booking Office (Monday–Saturday 8:00–20:00, Sunday 8:00–16:00, Kanal Griboyedova/Канал Грибоедова 24). This is across the canal from the Kazan Cathedral and just a few doors from Nevsky Prospekt. Look for the steam-engine sign above the building. Metro: Nevsky Prospekt/Невский Проспект.

Only Russian citizens are officially allowed to buy tickets from the windows in the main ground-floor hall. Foreigners should go to the right, then through the doorway to the right of the women's bathroom, following signs saying #100–104

Trains Departing St. Petersburg

#	To	Departs	Arrives	2nd Class	1st Class
37	Riga (Рига)	21:38	8:05	$45	$84
649	Tallinn (Таллинн)	23:10	8:16	$22	$40
191	Vilnius (Вильнюс)	17:52	6:20	$38	$68
33*	Helsinki (хельсинки)	7:00	12:30	$53	$92
35**	"	16:15	21:34	$53	$80
23	Moscow (Москва)	13:05	7:49	$33–$49***	$64–$72
159	"	16:00	21:43	$33–$49***	$64–$72
29	"	20:20	5:15	"	"
19	"	21:55	6:00	"	"
27	"	22:30	6:45	"	"
9	"	22:45	7:10	"	"
25	"	23:10	7:15	"	"
5	"(deluxe train)	23:33	7:45	"	"
1	"	23:55	8:25	"	"
3	"	23:59	8:30	"	"
13	"	0:35	10:03	"	"

* Russian-run *Repin*

** Finnish-run *Sibelius*

*** *Prices vary according to train, speed, and day of the week. Generally, the lower the number, the more expensive (and nicer) the train.*

and кассы международного сообщения. Most clerks do not speak English. They need to write your last name on the ticket in Cyrillic, and the easiest way to help them do this is to bring your passport and visa, but if you can't do that, any other ID (such as an American driver's license) is usually OK. Windows 100 through 104 sell in advance and same-day tickets to foreigners for destinations within the former Soviet Union, including the Baltic states. Round-trip tickets (e.g., to Moscow) are available if you purchase in advance. Students at Russian universities can visit windows 101 and 102 for lower rates. Window 94 sells tickets to Finland. If you have questions, window 90 is for information (75 cents per visit). To pay with a credit card, go to window 97. To get your money back on tickets you don't want, visit window 91. (These window numbers could change.)

If you don't want to brave the central booking office, Sindbad Travel at the St. Petersburg International Hostel can get tickets for you at a slight markup (see Hostels, above).

St. Petersburg to Helsinki: The Finnish-run Sibelius afternoon train is far more convenient than the Russian Repin. It's sleek, blue, and comfortable, and you can just hop on board and pay the conductor with a credit card, or in dollars or Finnish marks (although it's preferable, and slightly cheaper, to come a little early and buy a ticket at window 10 in the station). Since the Sibelius arrives in Helsinki in the evening, you should try to set up a place to stay by phone while in St. Petersburg.

The Russian-run Repin is not quite as nice as the Sibelius, though the price is the same. Since it leaves before the ticket windows open in the morning and since you can't pay on board, you have to buy your ticket the day before or earlier.

You can buy tickets for both trains from special windows at Finlyandskii Station itself, either in advance or on the day of departure. Walk two car-lengths up platform 1 and go in the door marked "Train tickets Express-2" in English. Window 9 sells tickets for the Russian train; window 10 sells tickets for the Finnish train (both windows daily 7:00–12:00 and 13:00–17:00). As tickets on these trains rarely sell out, it's enough to come the day of departure (for the Finnish train) or the day before (for the Russian train). If you prefer, you can also get tickets for these trains at the Central Railway Booking Office, window 94 (though not on the day of departure) or at Sindbad Travel at the St. Pete's Hostel.

St. Petersburg to Poland: There are daily direct trains from St. Petersburg to Warsaw and Berlin, but since these transit Latvia, Lithuania, and then Belarus, they are one long nightmare of customs and immigration checks, plus you may need various transit visas. Get to Poland instead from Moscow or the Baltics.

By Bus

St. Petersburg to Helsinki: The St. Petersburg Express Bus leaves St. Petersburg at 8:45 and arrives in Helsinki at 15:45.

Pick-ups in St. Petersburg are at 8:00 at the Hotel Pulkovskaya (near Metro: Moskovskaya/Московская), and 8:25 at Hotel Astoria (across from St. Isaac's), and 8:45 at Grand Hotel Europe. Make reservations at the Sovauto desk in the lobby of the Pulkovskaya (tel. 123-5125), or just show up. The bus continues from Helsinki to Turku port, meeting the Turku–Stockholm overnight ferries. Tickets to Helsinki cost $51, students 10 percent off.

The Pietarin Linja bus leaves St. Petersburg at 12:00 and arrives in Helsinki at 19:35 (no advance booking office, buy tickets from the driver). The bus departs daily from Hotel Moskva (Metro: pl. Aleksandra Nevskovo) at 12:00 and from Hotel Astoria at 12:30. Tickets $46, students 10 percent off.

Finnord buses leave St. Petersburg at 15:30 and 23:30, arriving in Helsinki at 21:45 and 06:30. They depart from the handy English-speaking office and waiting room at ulitsa Italyanskaya/Итальянская 37 (a half-block in from the Fontanka canal and a block from Nevsky Prospekt, Metro: Gostinii Dvor/Гостиныи Двор, tel. 314-8951, fax 314-7058 for reservations). Tickets $49, students 30 percent off.

St. Petersburg to Tallinn: Buses leave daily at 7:00 and 17:00 (arriving in Tallinn at 13:20 and 23:20) from platform 5 at Bus Station #2 (naberezhnaya Obvodnovo Kanala/Обводного Канала 36). Exit Metro: Ligovskii Prospekt/Лиговский Проспект, then go one tram stop south (just across the canal), and 1.5 blocks east along the canal. Or take a cab. Buy tickets inside the station for $11.

By Air
Connections between the Airport and Downtown: St. Petersburg's Pulkovo airport has two terminals. Pulkovo-I handles domestic flights and Pulkovo-II handles international flights. To reach either from downtown St. Petersburg, first take the Metro to the Moskovskaya/Московская station, take the exit on the outbound end of the station, and go all the way through the underground tunnel. This will bring you out next to the stops for bus #13 (which goes to Pulkovo-II) and bus #39 (which goes to Pulkovo-I). At peak times bus #13 runs every 20 minutes. Since Pulkovo-II is not the end of bus #13's route, there are both inbound and outbound bus stops at the airport (marked by yellow signs). If you've just landed and need to take the bus into town, stand at the inbound stop (near the arrivals hall).

For booking and reconfirmation: You can visit major airlines' downtown offices such as British Airways, Nevsky Prospekt 57, tel. 325-6222; Delta, Bolshaya Morskaya ulitsa 36, tel. 311-5820; Finnair, Malaya Morskaya ulitsa 19, tel. 325-9500; LOT, Karavannaya ulitsa 1, tel. 273-5721; Malev, Voznesenskii pr. 7, tel. 315-5455; Swissair, Nevsky Prospekt 57, tel. 325-3250; Austrian Air, Nevsky Prospekt 57, tel. 325-3260; and SAS, Nevsky Prospekt 57, tel. 325-3255.

TALLINN, ESTONIA

Tallinn is the flagship of Baltic reform. During the Soviet era, Tallinners spent their evenings watching Finnish television beamed across the gulf from Helsinki. When independence came, they knew exactly what a Western economy should look like. Since 1991 they've been putting one together as fast as possible. If only everyone in the ex-Soviet Union could learn from the Estonians.

Walk into any grocery store and you'll understand. The stores carry a sensible mix of imported and domestic goods, just like any other store in Europe. Estonian design has recovered from Sovietism—colorful, simple, Scandinavian layout is showing up in airline ads and yogurt packaging. And Estonia's competitive trade policy is producing competitive goods: while Russian exports to Estonia have sunk, in St. Petersburg you can now pick up Estonian orange juice, cucumbers, and frozen fish. This little country is succeeding.

Why the economic precociousness? One main reason is that Estonians consider their country a Nordic nation of solid, hardworking Protestant folk like those who made Scandinavia a showcase of order, propriety, and comfort. They're quick to point out that Finland and Estonia both gained independence from Russia after World War I and that as late as 1938, Estonia's living standard was equal to Finland's. Estonians would have kept up had it not been for a couple hundred Russian tanks.

Of course, well-stocked grocery stores look perfectly

normal if you come to Tallinn on the boat from Helsinki. This is why I suggest that you arrive in Tallinn from Russia or one of the other Baltic capitals. You'll feel like you're back in the West already. Coming from Helsinki, Tallinn looks run-down. Remember that it gets worse, and enjoy Tallinn while you can.

Planning Your Time

Tallinn deserves more time than Riga or Vilnius. But it's fairly small and its sights are modest. Rather, it steadily delivers small and pleasing towers, museums, ramparts, facades, churches, and shops. Wander through the Old Town, have a Saku beer in the square, duck down every street and into every shop that looks interesting, and peer up at the Hanseatic facades and medieval towers. On a first trip, two days are plenty.

Day 1

11:00 Wander through the Old Town, looking out for concert posters on your way up to Toompea, Tallinn's fortified hill.

12:30 Leisurely lunch at Toomkooli.

14:00 Go down to Kiek in de Kök and see the photography exhibitions.

15:00 Explore the small galleries and shops in the Old Town. Stop in any café when you want a rest.

19:00 Concerts usually take place at this time. Come a little early for tickets.

20:30 Dinner at Eesli Tall.

22:00 Retire to Hell Hunt or the Eesli Tall cellar bar.

Day 2

10:00 Check out the Holy Ghost Church and perhaps the Tallinn Town Museum or the Estonian History Museum.

12:00 Assemble picnic fixings at the Kaubahall supermarket. Take the tram out to Kadriorg.

13:30 Picnic and walk through the Kadriorg park and palace grounds.

18:00 Return to the Old Town for dinner at Vanaema Juures (make reservations ahead of time).

20:00 Plenty of time for mulled wine at the Virgin Tower.

Tallinn

Orientation

Tallinn owes its existence to Toompea, the precipitous hill on which the city's Upper Town stands. Fortified by the Danes after they captured Tallinn in 1219, Toompea turned into Tallinn's aristocratic neighborhood during the later Middle Ages—Toompea Castle still houses the Estonian government. Merchants and artisans, meanwhile, built the other half of old Tallinn, the Lower Town, beneath Toompea. Two steep, narrow streets—the "Long Leg" (Pikk jalg) and the "Short Leg" (Lühike jalg)—connect the two towns. Tallinn's intact city wall counts 29 watchtowers, each topped by a pointy red roof. Nineteenth- and early 20th-century architects circled the Old Town, putting up broad streets of public buildings, low Scandinavian-style apartment buildings, and single-family wooden houses. Soviet planners then ringed this with stands of crumbling concrete high-rises where many of Tallinn's Russian immigrants settled. The Town Hall Square (Raekoja plats), in the center of the Lower Town, is an important reference point.

Tourist Information: Tallinn's excellent, English-speaking tourist office has maps, concert listings, booklets, phrase books, postcards, and free brochures. Pick up a copy of *Tallinn This Week* (Monday–Friday 9:00–19:00, Saturday–Sunday 10:00–17:00; closing an hour early off-season; on the main square, Raekoja plats 10, tel. 631-3940, fax 631-3941, Web site: www.tallinn.ee, e-mail: tallinn@netexpress.ee).

American Embassy: Kentmanni 20, third floor, tel. 631-2021.

Bookstore: Homeros carries books exclusively in foreign languages, including English. It doesn't have a very big selection, but it's worth visiting (Monday–Friday 10:00–19:00, Saturday–Sunday 11:00–17:00, Vene 20).

Laundry: Seebimull Pesumaja, a self-service and drop-off Laundromat, is at Liivalaia 7 (1 block east of Pärnu maantee at the intersection with Suda, tel. 2/682-010).

Currency Exchange
14 Estonian kroons (kr) = about $1, 1 kroon = 100 senti
There are booths everywhere. Banks have the best rates—look for a 1 to 1.5 percent spread between buying and selling prices. A 1 percent commission on traveler's checks is standard. A lot of change points, like those in major hotels, have very poor rates, so shop around. The American Express representative is at Suur-Karja 15 in the Old Town (Monday–Friday 9:00–18:00, Saturday 10:00–17:00).

Telephones and Mail
Both the phone and post offices are in the fortress-like building on Narva maantee across from the Hotel Viru. Send letters from the second-floor post office (Monday–Friday 8:00–19:00, Saturday 9:00–17:00). For long-distance calls, the office on the lower floor of the post office building is open daily from 7:30 to 20:00. The best way to call is with phone cards (in 30-kr, 50-kr, and 100-kr sizes) sold in the telephone office and around town. These work in Estonia's new card phones. Calls to Helsinki, Riga, and Vilnius cost 5 kr per minute; to Russia and Sweden, 7.5 kr; to America, 16 kr. Local calls from new card-operated phones cost 24 senti.

Tallinn has two types of telephone numbers. The seven-digit ones have no area code and always begin with 6, like this: 632-3232. The six-digit numbers have an area code (2) which we always list before the number, like this: 2/454-454. Calling within the city, you dial all seven digits of the numbers that begin with 6, but only the last six digits of the numbers that begin with 2. Making a long-distance or international call to Tallinn, always dial the full seven numbers, including the 2 before six-digit numbers.

Getting Around Tallinn

Unless you're sleeping far from the center, you should be able to do most of your sightseeing on foot. Tallinn's trams are very simple and convenient. Check the map for route and stop locations. All trams meet in the center, by the Hotel Viru. They run until about midnight. One of the easiest ways to get around Tallinn is to spend $4.50 on a ten-day card (*10-päeva-kaart*) which gives you unlimited rides on public transport in Tallinn. Cards and tickets are sold near tram stops at the kiosks that say *sõidutalongid* in the window. You can also get single tickets for 4 kr from the booths or on board. Some buses are run by a private company called MRP (they have a three-triangle logo); these cost 6 kr per ride and passes are not valid.

Taxis are cheap and handy in Tallinn. Always make sure to take an official taxi. The largest, cheapest, and most reliable taxi company is Tulika Takso; the best way to summon them is to call 654-1959.

Sights—Tallinn's Toompea

This is the fortified hill where Tallinn was founded in the 13th century and the Upper Town was built. Walk up Nunne tänav, the street that leads from the train station to the Old Town, then cut off to the right and climb up the stairs. The ramparts at the top reward you with a perfect photo opportunity of the Lower Town's red roofs and steeples. Wandering will bring you to the **Dome Church** (Toomkirik) and eventually out to the square by the colorful **Russian Orthodox Church** (built by Alexander Nevsky in 1894), a plump, out-of-place, onion-domed edifice planted here well after the Russian takeover of Tallinn in 1710. The interior is worth a peek.

Downhill from the church you'll see two towers. The square **Virgin Tower** (Neitsitorn) houses a café; the round one is **Kiek in de Kök** ("Peek in the Kitchen"), so named because one could supposedly spy on the Lower Town's residents from its heights. The top floor and the bottom two

Tallinn's Old Town

floors now house changing exhibits of the latest in Estonian photography, while in the middle you can see medieval cannons and charts left over from the Livonian wars (7 kr, students 3.50 kr, Tuesday, Wednesday, and Friday 10:30–17:30, Saturday–Sunday 11:00–16:00). If you head back down to the Lower Town from here you'll pass by **St. Nicholas' Church** (Niguliste Kirik) and the World War II ruins behind it, left untouched as a memorial.

▲**Estonian Art Museum** (Eesti Kunstimuuseum)—Shouldn't be your first stop in town, but if you're interested in late

19th- and early 20th-century art, go check out what the Estonians were doing (10 kr, students 3 kr, Wednesday–Monday 11:00–17:30, closed Tuesday, Kiriku plats 1, on Toompea).

Sights—Tallinn's Lower Town

▲**Walking Tours**—Walking tours of the Old Town are offered daily at 14:00 mid-May through mid-September (50 kr/person, 1.5 hrs, ask at CDS Reisid on Raekoja plats 17, tel. 627-6797, fax 631-3666). To hire a private guide, ask at CDS or the tourist office.

▲▲**Holy Ghost Church** (Pühavaimu Kirik)—This quintessentially northern 14th-century church has a fantastic old outdoor clock. Inside, hunched, whitewashed walls contrast with the faded medieval artwork on aged pews and galleries. Watch for periodic organ concerts (at Pühavaimu tänav and Pikk tänav across from the Maiasmokk café).

▲**Estonian History Museum** (Eesti Ajaloomuuseum)— Quite varied exhibits, so you may be able to find something to hold your interest among archaeology, military history, a roomful of domestic displays, and more. Look for the English captions on the sides of the glass cases. The building is Tallinn's 15th-century Great Guildhall (5 kr, Thursday–Tuesday 11:00–18:00, closed Wednesday, Pikk 17, across from the Holy Ghost Church).

▲**Tallinn Town Museum** (Tallinna Linnamuuseum)— Features Tallinn history from 1700 to 1918, with the upstairs exhibit on Tallinn from 1900 to 1917 the best part. The mixture of Russian, German, and Estonian reminds us that the ethnic situation here was once even more complicated than it now is (5 kr, students 2.50 kr, Wednesday–Monday 10:30–17:30, closed Tuesday, Vene 17 at the corner of Pühavaimu).

▲**Estonian Maritime Museum** (Eesti Meremuuseum)— Housed in the Paks Margareeta ("Fat Margaret") tower, the museum itself is less interesting than the view of Tallinn's port if you go out the wooden door on the top floor and up to the tower roof. It's scary to think that anyone might have ever used the suit of copper diving armor, built by a Tallinner in the 1920s, that stands in a corner of the bottom floor (6 kr, students 2 kr, Wednesday–Sunday 10:00–18:00, closed Monday and Tuesday, Pikk 70).

▲▲**Artwork, handicrafts, and shopping**—With so many Scandinavian tourists coming to Tallinn, the Old Town is full of trinkets. For sweaters and woolens, try the **Gallerii Kaks** (Monday–Friday 11:00–19:00, weekends 10:00–18:00, on the second floor of Lühike jalg 1). **Diele Gallerii** sells the best postcards in town, displays work by Estonian artists, and has some nice art for sale (at Vanaturu kael 3 just below Raekoja plats). Also check out the **Kinaver** ceramics store on Toompea at Pikk jalg 9, next to what must be the cleanest public bathrooms in the ex-Soviet Union (4 kr). The **Tallinn Department Store** (Tallinna Kaubamaja) is behind the Hotel Viru (Monday–Saturday 9:00–20:00, Sunday 10:00–18:00) and the **Stockmann** department store is a little farther away, at Liivalaia 53.

Outside the Center

▲▲**Kadriorg**—This seaside park and summer residence was built by Peter the Great for Catherine after Russia took over Tallinn in 1710. The mansion is below the home of the president of Estonia. The park, which runs down to the sea to the north, is the perfect spot for your picnic. The permanent tram, set up as a diner outside the entrance, is also a fun place to eat. Trams #1 and #3 go east from the center of Tallinn to Kadriorg at the end of the line (where the tram makes a U-turn). It's an easy 15-minute ride out and back.

Music in Tallinn

Tallinn has one of the densest per-capita schedules of Baroque, Renaissance, and choral music performances in Northern Europe. Estonian choral music got its first push from the long German Lutheran presence in Tallinn, and then became intimately bound up with the struggle for independence after the first Estonian Song Festival in 1869 (which is still held every five years; next one in 1999). Even outside of festival times, it's a rare week in which there aren't a few performances in Tallinn's churches and concert halls, advertised on posters around town ("Hortus Musicus" is the name of Estonia's best-known Renaissance music performance group). In most cases tickets are available either at the door or in advance from the Eesti Kontsert ticket office inside the big theater (Monday–Saturday 13:00–19:00, Estonia puiestee 4, across the park from the Hotel Viru). Estonian groups have put out a lot of good CDs, and the place to look for them is the record shop at Kuninga 4, around the corner from

Raekoja plats (Monday–Friday 9:00–19:00, Saturday 9:00–17:00). Estonia's three best modern choral composers and arrangers are Arvo Pärt, Veljo Tormis, and Erkki-Sven Tüür.

Sleeping in Tallinn
(14 kr = about $1)
If you're calling from the U.S.A., dial 011-372, then the local number; for more phone info, see the Appendix: Dialing Direct Within Russia & the Baltics.

Respectable Hotels
Hotell Mihkli delivers actual respectability at the best rates in town. This means newish furniture, functioning bathrooms, locked parking, a TV, phone, and nice writing desk in every room, and a welcoming reception desk. With breakfast and sauna included, singles cost 600 kr and doubles are 850 kr (Visa, MasterCard, and American Express accepted). It's past the National Library a little outside the center, about a 15-minute walk downhill from Toompea. From the station, take trolley #4 to the "Endla" stop—the hotel is a 5-minute walk (Endla 23, EE0001 Tallinn, tel. 2/453-704, fax 2/451-767).

Hotell Central is a little more expensive, but the location lives up to the name and the rooms are very new. Singles are 880 kr, doubles are 990 kr, and breakfast is included (Narva maantee 7, EE0001 Tallinn, tel. 633-9800, fax 633-9900).

Hotel Nepi, with comfy public areas, is a small, friendly, family-run hotel a short bus ride from the center (bus 17 or 17A) where singles with bath cost 400 kr, doubles 500 kr, and breakfast 50 kr per person. It's about a 50-kr taxi ride from the ferry port (Nepi 10, EE0013 Tallinn, tel. 655-1665, fax 655-1664).

Hotell Kristiine just makes it into the "respectable" category. This is the cheapest hotel in town where you can have a private bathroom. The rooms are standard-issue Soviet style on several floors of a taller building, well-kept but with older furniture, TVs, and telephones. Each room has a small, spartan private bathroom. The reception is well-organized and speaks English. Singles with bath and breakfast cost 370 kr, doubles are 460 kr, triples 580 kr. Take tram #3 or #4 to the "Vineeri" stop at the corner of Pärnu maantee and Luha tänav; the hotel is about 3 blocks down Luha at #16 (EE0001 Tallinn, tel. 2/682-000, fax 646-1329).

Cheaper Hotels and Hostels

The Barn (Hotell Küün), centrally located 1 block off the town square, is Tallinn's hostel. Everyone speaks English. There's space for 36 people in several big rooms with new blondwood beds (dorm bed 160 kr, doubles 495 kr, 10 percent off for hostel members, breakfast not included, Väike-Karja 1, EE0001 Tallinn, tel. 2/443-465). The adjacent Erootika Bar looks like it's affiliated with the hostel, but it's not.

At **Hotell Dorell**, double rooms with clean shared bathrooms cost 460 kr (breakfast not included). Don't expect much English or warmth. Take tram line #1 or #3 to the "Kreutzwaldi" stop, just east of the city center along Narva maantee. When you get off the tram, go through the archway at Narva maantee 23 and you'll see the hotel sign to your left (Karu 39, EE0001 Tallinn, tel. 626-1200, fax 2/423-387).

University dorms open up in summer for backpackers. You'll pay about 80 kr for a bed in a three-bed room. Ask at the tourist office for details.

Private Rooms

Tallinn has two separate agencies which will find you a room with a local family. They're both fine and you should just go to the one that's most convenient to wherever you arrive. Fairly few people actually live in the Old Town in Tallinn, so very few private rooms are in the old section, though many are within walking distance.

At **CDS Reisid**, singles go for 295 kr and doubles for 445 kr (breakfast included). If you reserve ahead, they can pick you up at the train station, ferry port, or airport for 95 kr, though it's cheaper to just take a taxi (Monday–Friday 9:00–19:00 and weekends 10:00–16:00, Raekoja plats 17, second floor, next to tourist office and above the Kangur shop, tel. 627-6797, fax 631-3666.)

Rasastra is convenient for those arriving by sea (though if you reserve in advance, they'll also pick you up at the train station or airport). This office is just up the street, on the right as you exit the ferry terminal (daily 10:00–18:00, Sadama 11, tel. & fax 2/602-091). Singles cost 150 kr–235 kr and doubles range from 260 kr–410 kr, depending on location. The optional breakfast costs 25 kr.

Host Family Association also arranges homestays in Tallinn as well as Moscow, St. Petersburg, Riga, and Vilnius ($30 for one person, $50 for two, or $60 single/$90 double with all meals, tel. & fax 7/812/275-1992 in St. Petersburg, e-mail: alexei@hofak.hop.stu.neva.ru).

Eating in Tallinn

It's easy to get a good meal for $10 in Tallinn. Dozens of restaurants have opened in the Old Town in the past few years, often in cozy medieval cellars. Estonian cuisine is a satisfying northern mixture of meat, potatoes, root vegetables, and soups, with some seafood now and then. Estonia's Saku beer has an excellent reputation. Blue-labeled Saku Originaal is the most widely drunk, but some prefer darker Saku Tume. Saku Vichy and Värska are Estonia's main bottled water brands. Most restaurants accept credit cards.

Few restaurants can match **Eesli Tall** (the "Donkey Stable") for stability and convenience—it's been the most reliable dining choice in Tallinn for over five years. Everyone goes there, and so will you—expect crowds on summer weekends. The atmosphere in the upstairs section is soothing and candlelit, and there are vegetarian options on the menu. The downstairs is half-bar, half-restaurant, dungeon-walled and whitewashed, a maze of tunnels, archways, and hidden rooms. Meals cost 100 kr to 150 kr and beer goes for 26 kr (Sunday–Thursday 11:00–02:00, Friday–Saturday 11:00–04:00, Dunkri 4/6, just uphill from the Town Hall, tel. 631-3755).

Vanaema Juures (which translates roughly as "Chez Grandma") is a small cellar restaurant which really is decorated like your grandmother's dining room—family portraits, a grandfather clock, and grandfather's attempts at painting. Enjoy homey, candlelit meals (e.g., pork roast with sauerkraut and juniper berries). Entrees run 85 kr to 105 kr, and dinner reservations are strongly advised (Monday–Saturday 12:00–23:00, Sunday 12:00–18:00, Rataskaevu 10, tel. 631-3929).

Toomkooli serves the best fair-priced square meal on Toompea (most entrees 90–150 kr). The menu is heavy on meat, potatoes, mushrooms, and sausage. Consider reservations (daily 12:00–23:00, Toomkooli 13, on the west edge of Toompea, tel. 2/446-613).

Teater Restoran is a typical cellar restaurant with a rabbit warren of small rooms. On a cold day, order pancakes with

cream and ask to sit by the fireplace. Set menus for 70 kr are
the best reason to come here (daily 9:00–01:00, Lai 31, near
Oleviste church, tel. 631-4518).

Ai Sha Ni Ya is a real Chinese restaurant with reasonable prices, a relaxing atmosphere, and chopsticks on your
table. Most of the dishes are bland because Estonians aren't
used to spicy food (daily 12:00–24:00, Mere puiestee 6, up a
driveway from the street in a courtyard, tel. 2/441-997).

Peetri Pizza is a chain with several branches in Tallinn.
The Francescana pizza is good (34 kr per large one-person
pizza). The branch on Lai 4 has only a few seats but is just
steps from the Town Hall Square (10:00–21:00). The branch
at Kopli 2c (enter from Vana-Kalamaja) is right by the train
station, in the building on the corner across from the tram stop
(daily 11:00–22:00). The take-out-only branch by the tram
stop at Pärnu maantee 22, near the Palace Hotel, is open from
10:00 to 02:00 in the morning (weather depending), and takes
phone orders at 2/666-711.

For a less casual sit-down pizza meal, the best place is
Pizza Americana on Harju at the corner of Müürivahe, by the
WWII ruins.

Cafés: The **Maiasmokk** café and pastry shop (founded
in 1864) is the grande dame of Tallinn cafés, and a tasty
place for breakfast if you're staying at the Barn. Just point to
what you want at the pastry counter, or sit down for breakfast or coffee on the other side of the shop. Everything's very
cheap (daily 11:00–22:00, Pikk 16, across from the church
with the old clock). **Hõbekass** is a larger café where you can
linger and talk. There are plenty of tables in two rooms, with
decent pastries and light meals (Monday–Friday 8:00–22:00,
Saturday–Sunday 10:00–22:00, Harju 7, across from the
World War II ruins).

For the café with the best view, try the **Neitsitorn** (Virgin Tower), the square, many-windowed tower next to Kiek in
de Kök. The service and selection are still a little Soviet, but
the top two floors overlook the Lower Town and serve hors
d'oeuvres, pastries, and mineral water. In summer there's
sometimes live classical music on the outdoor terrace. The
ground floor serves hot mulled wine (*hõõgvein*) out of wooden
casks for 12 kr per half-glass (daily 11:00–22:00).

These days it can seem like all Tallinn is one large
Finnish nightclub, but a couple favorite spots are **Hell Hunt**,

an Irish-style pub at Pikk 39, the **Von Krahli** at Rataskaevu 10, and the **Nimeta** bar at Suur-Karja 4/6.

For **picnics,** just about every neighborhood in Tallinn has a grocery store. The convenient **Kaubahall** supermarket is in the center of town (Monday–Saturday 9:00–20:30, Sunday 9:00–20:00, Aia 7, not far from the twin Viru towers). The **Lembitukaubamaja,** across the bus lot from the Hotel Viru, is a smaller store open daily until 23:00.

Near Tallinn: Tartu

The obvious day trip from Tallinn is to Tartu, Estonia's university town. Tartu's old city is built in a newer, classical style no less pleasing than Tallinn's Hanseatic center. Tartu has not managed Tallinn's commercial boom. You can put together a picnic at the Tartu Turg (market) in the center of town, then eat it on the banks of the Emajõgi River, which runs along the east side of the Old Town. Or head to the west, above the Old Town, to the set of bluffs where Tartu's ruined cathedral (partly rebuilt into an excellent museum) and early university buildings stand. The peeling paint of the 19th-century wooden houses that ring the old city, the ravines that cut through the bluffs, and the smell of coal-fired heating make parts of Tartu resemble a Massachusetts mill town.

Buses to Tartu leave roughly hourly from the Tallinn bus station between 6:00 and 21:00, take 2.5 hours, and cost 70 kr one-way.

If you have time for a one- or two-night trip out of Tallinn and want to see the countryside, go to one of Estonia's

Trains Departing Tallinn

#	To	Leaves	Arrives	2nd Class	1st Class
IK4	Moscow (Moskva)	17:50	10:08	508 kr	993 kr
R120	St. Petersburg (Peterburi)	20:10	6:54	204 kr	411 kr
IK2	Warsaw* (Varssavi)	17:20	13:26	663 kr	1,054 kr
*via Riga, Kaunas, and Šeštokai					

big islands—Saaremaa or Hiiumaa. Buses take you from Tallinn to the coast at Virtsu, and then by ferry to Kuressaare, the largest town on Saaremaa, in about five hours for 100 kr. The Tallinn tourist office can give you advice on booking accommodations on the islands.

Transportation Connections—Tallinn

By Train
The Tallinn train station (Balti jaam) is a short walk from the Old Town along Nunne tänav and a short, simple ride from the Hotel Viru by trams #1 or #2 (4 kr, buy at booth or on board). This is the smallest, cleanest, and best-organized station in the Baltics, with few lines and fairly simple procedures. The station has two parts: a smaller hall, at the head of the tracks, and a larger hall, which runs alongside the tracks. The small hall is for suburban commuter trains.

Advance purchase windows for international trains (including trains to Russia) are upstairs on the second floor of the large hall. On the ground floor, you'll find currency exchange, an English-speaking *informatsioon* window (daily 6:30–22:30), and windows 5 and 6, where you can purchase tickets for trains leaving the same day or return tickets for refunds. Window 5 also processes phoned-in reservations (tel. 615-6632).

By Bus
Tallinn's bus station (Autobussijaam) is off Tartu maantee at Lastekodu 46, too far from the center to walk comfortably. Take tram #2 or #4 east from the city center to the "Bussi-jaam" stop, then turn the corner to your right (see our map). Buy tickets at the station.

Most long-distance buses to and from Tallinn also stop at the Reisisadam ferry terminal either just before or just after the bus station. Check with the driver or the station personnel to make sure.

Tallinn to Riga: In summer 1997, buses to Riga left at 7:00, 10:00, 12:15, 13:15, 15:00, 19:45, 22:35, and 23:40, arriving in Riga at 11:40, 15:35, 17:40, 18:15, 21:05, 01:25, 03:45, and 05:40. Fares were 132 kr. Some buses are nonstop, some aren't (for example, the 15:00 bus, which continues to Vilnius, doesn't stop between Tallinn and Riga).

Tallinn to Vilnius: Buses to Vilnius left daily at 12:15 and 22:35, arriving at 22:30 and 9:00, respectively. Tickets cost 256 kr.

Tallinn to St. Petersburg: Buses left at 7:30 and 14:30, arriving at 15:25 and 22:25 St. Petersburg time (an hour ahead of Tallinn) for 150 kr.

By Boat

The **Reisisadam** (main ferry port) in Tallinn is at the end of Sadama tänav, about a 20-minute walk from the town square. MRP bus 88 and 92 will take you from the port to the Hotel Viru for 6 kr. Trams #1 and #2 also stop five minutes from the port at the base of Sadama tänav, and you can call for a taxi. There are four terminal buildings at the port (A, B, C, and D). The different ferry companies' signs will help you find the right one.

In 1997 Tallink hydrofoils docked at the separate **Linna-hall** terminal, about five to ten minutes' walk west from the Reisisadam and even closer to the town square.

See the Gateways chapter for full fare and schedule details on sailings to Helsinki and Stockholm. The best way to reserve a place on a ship leaving Tallinn is to phone the ferry companies during business hours (Estline tel. 631-3636, Tallink 640-9808, Viking 631-8193, Eestin Linjat 631-8606, Silja 631-8331). You can also visit any travel agent in town; stop by the ferry companies' downtown offices (e.g., the Estline office at Aia 5a); or come to the port, where ticket offices are open whenever ships sail.

By Air

Connections between the Airport and Downtown:
Tallinn's airport is the best of the five cities in this book. MRP bus 2 runs between the airport and the center of town for 6 kr. The airport is quite close in, and fair taxi drivers using the meter will charge no more than about 40 kr to the center.

For booking and reconfirmation: Either go to the airport or the Lufthansa City Center office at Pärnu maantee 10 (Monday–Friday 9:00–18:00, Saturday 10:00–15:00, tel. 2/444-037 or 631-4444, fax 631-3566).

RIGA, LATVIA

Tall 19th- and 20th-century buildings give Riga a cosmopolitan feel and a vertical accent unique among the Baltic capitals. Bishop Albert of Bremen, German merchants, and the Teutonic Knights made Riga the center of Baltic Christianization, commercialization, and colonization when they founded the city in the early 1200s. Under the czars, the city was the Russian Empire's busiest commercial port. Under Soviet rule, Riga became first an important military center and later, because of its high standard of living, one of the favored places for high-ranking military officers to retire to (they were given a choice of anywhere in the U.S.S.R. except Moscow, Kiev, and St. Petersburg). The Soviets encouraged Russian immigration and the percentage of residents who were Latvian plunged from well over half to about a third today.

The result is that although all the street signs are now in Latvian only, life in Riga goes on in two languages. Lithuanian and Estonian dominate Vilnius and Tallinn despite large Russian and Polish minorities, but in Riga you'll hear Russian on the street just as much as Latvian. Latvia's major newspapers, such as the daily *Diena*, come out in dual Russian and Latvian editions. And Lutheranism notwithstanding, Riga is the most Soviet-feeling Baltic capital city. It has not visibly Westernized itself as much as Tallinn. Still, Riga is far ahead of most of the former Soviet Union on the road to economic viability, and what it has done has muscle. The Latvian lat is rock-solid, and with Riga the largest city in the Baltics some predict that it is on the verge of an economic boom that will outstrip Tallinn.

Riga's Old Town is the least medieval in the Baltics. The big churches, the moat, the bastion, fragments of the city walls, a couple dozen houses, and the cannonballs embedded in the Powder Tower are all that survive from the Middle Ages. Much of the Old Town is in 18th-century classical style; the rest of the center, and almost all of the newer parts that immediately ring it, are fine examples of late 19th- and early 20th-century building styles, particularly the Art Nouveau (Jugendstil) that betrays Riga's connections to the German-speaking world. Emerging from the Soviet period, many of these buildings no longer have quite enough warmth and life to fill their once-elegant, high-ceilinged rooms. But they are still very nice to look at. The best way to do this is to walk along the streets near the parks (such as Elizabetes iela and Alberta iela) and around the city's main commercial artery—Brīvības iela—which starts by the Freedom Monument and runs away from the Old Town and the Daugava River.

The Latvian ethnic mix is potentially the Baltics' most explosive. Russian-speakers make up about 45 percent of Latvia's population, and a majority of Riga's. Very few of them have become Latvian citizens. Yet most Russians don't want to leave; they like life in the Baltics better than life in their supposed homeland. Although it gets more media attention, the situation in Estonia is calmer and closer to being resolved. There are fewer Russians in Estonia than in Latvia, and Estonia has done a better job of trying to integrate them into Estonian society.

It is impossible to do justice to the Baltic Russian issue in just a few paragraphs, but Anatol Lieven discusses the problem thoroughly and evenhandedly in his book *The Baltic Revolution*. As a traveler, you may sense that the issue gets blown out of proportion. You will see very little Russian-Latvian and Russian-Estonian friction. Most of the service personnel in stores in Tallinn and Riga seem to switch effortlessly and naturally from one language to the next.

Perhaps the most important point in the Russo-Baltic debate is that regardless of their citizenship, residents of the Baltics enjoy clean streets, well-stocked grocery stores, stable currencies, and a far better standard of living than residents in Russia. The improvement in the Baltics is a direct result of the end of Russian and Soviet domination. And ultimately, economic

Riga

health is probably a prerequisite for a generous resolution of the Baltic states' ethnic questions. Estonians and Latvians must be puzzled to see that in most of Finland, with a Swedish population of only 6 percent, all public signs and services are bilingual. Estonia and Latvia, with Russian-speaking populations of 30 and 45 percent, respectively, are in full retreat from official bilingualism. The difference, of course, is that Sweden is no longer an aggressive colonizing nation, while Finns have a sense of prosperity and national security that overshadows any "threat" from the Swedes in their midst. One can only hope that the Baltics' future will be equally as calm.

Planning Your Time
Like Tallinn, Riga is worth two days but, for most, no more.

Day 1
10:00 Go up St. Peter's Church for a look around Riga.

12:00 Grab a sandwich at Fredis.
13:00 Learn your way around the Old Town, visiting the
       Dom, the Museum of the History of Riga, and the
       Occupation Museum, and buy concert tickets if there's
       anything you want to hear.
18:00 Dinner at one of the restaurants in Dome Square.

Day 2
10:00 Explore Riga's central market.
12:00 Go to the Hare Krishna café, Osiris, or Pizzeria Lulu
       for lunch.
14:00 Walk along Elizabetes iela to Alberta iela, looking at the
       Jugendstil architecture, and then visit the Art
       Museum.
16:30 Extra time for another museum or another look around
       the Old Town.
18:00 Dinner at Rozamunde or Vērdiņš.

Orientation

Riga's Old Town is on the right bank of the Daugava, which is
very wide and crossed by three car bridges. The bus and train
stations and most sights, shops, and services are either in the
Old Town or in the 19th-century section of town immediately
around it. You should never need to venture across the river,
unless you wind up sleeping there.

Tourist Information: The tourist office (Rīgas Tūrisma
Informācijas Birojs), next to St. Peter's Church, is at Skārņu
iela 22 (daily 9:00–19:00, tel. 722-1731, fax 722-7680). It
hands out free brochures and sells maps and the handy information booklet *Riga In Your Pocket* (50 santims, also available
at kiosks or newsstands, or free at American Express if you're
lucky). It has all the in-depth info on Riga that this book
doesn't have the space to cover, as well as good street and
transport maps. It's updated every two months. The errati-
cally available *Riga This Week* is not worth buying, but you
may be able to pick it up for free.

American Embassy: Raiņa bulvāris 7, tel. 721-0005.

Bookstore: Aperto Libro is an English-language bookstore with a small stock including Baltic history, maps, fiction, textbooks, and dictionaries (Monday 10:00–19:00,
Tuesday–Saturday 10:00–20:00, Kr. Barona iela 31, tel. 728-
3810). Nearby, **Jāņa sēta** at Elizabetes iela 83/85 is the place

for maps and guidebooks (Monday–Friday 10:00–19:00, Saturday 11:00–17:00).

Laundry: The Miele Laundromat, through the archway at Elizabetes iela 85a (near Kr. Barona iela), is a savior for travelers in the Baltics. Two blocks from the train station, it has brand-new German machines and a café. Self-service costs 2.52 lats (Ls) per large load, full-service 4.72 Ls (open 24 hours, less busy on weekdays, tel. 721-7696).

Currency Exchange
0.6 lats (Ls) = about $1, 1 lat = 100 santims (s)

It's available everywhere. Rates are very competitive, so don't settle for more than a 1 percent spread between buying and selling rates. Two banks near the Dom that change American Express checks are Rīgas Komercbanka at Smilšu iela 6 and the Deutsch-Lettische Bank at Jēkaba iela 3/5. Latvia Tours is American Express' representative (Monday–Friday 9:00-18:00, Ka__u 8, tel. 721-3652).

Telephones and Mail
There is a 24-hour telephone-and-post office (with an ATM) catty-corner from the Freedom Monument at Brīvības iela 19 (open 24 hours) and another branch at the train station. These offices and many stores will sell you the telephone cards (smallest denomination 2 Ls) that work in Riga's abundant new pay phones.

Telephone numbers in Riga come in two types: old numbers that start with 2 and new numbers that start with 7. If the phone number of the phone you're calling from starts with 7, you always dial the full seven digits of the number you're calling. If you're calling from a number that starts with 2 to another number that starts with 2, dial only the six digits following the 2; from a 2-number to a 7-number, dial 1, then the full seven digits.

Numbers beginning with 2 are speedily being converted to 7-numbers as the Latvian phone system goes digital, and by the time you read this, the handful of 2-numbers listed in this book may have changed. Check the latest edition of *Riga In Your Pocket*.

Getting Around Riga
Tickets for Riga's buses, trams, and trolleybuses are sold at kiosks (and by drivers) for 14 s apiece. If you are staying in

the center, you can walk almost everywhere. Call 070 for a
taxi. Rides around the center of town should cost between
0.50 and 1.50 Ls.

Sights—Riga

▲▲▲**State Museum of Latvian Art** (Latvijas valsts mākslas
muzejs)—This is the best art museum in the Baltics. The grand
staircase is impressive, but especially worthwhile is the permanent exhibition of Latvian art on the second floor. The collection, almost entirely from 1910 to 1940, concentrates all the
artistic and political influences that stirred Latvia then: French
impressionism, German design, and Russian propaganda-
poster style on the one hand; European internationalism, Latvian nationalism, rural romanticism, and Communism on the
other. Check out the Russian art on the first floor if you won't
make it to St. Petersburg (Wednesday–Monday 11:00–17:00,
closed Tuesday, Kr. Valdemāra iela 10a).

▲▲▲**Occupation Museum** (Latvijas 50 gadu okupācijas
muzeja fonds)—A very complete exhibit covering Latvian history from 1940 to 1990, particularly the deportation of Latvians to Siberia: you can step into a replica of a gulag barracks
and see prisoners' letters home written on strips of birchbark.
Don't expect a balanced and self-critical presentation; this is a
pro-Latvian place. Full English captions. Free, but donations
accepted (Tuesday–Friday and Sunday 11:00–17:00, closed
Monday and Saturday, Strēlnieku laukums 1, near where Kaļķu
iela meets the river).

▲▲**Freedom Monument** (Brīvības piemniekelis)—Dedicated
in 1935, located on a traffic island in the middle of Brīvības
iela, this monument was strangely left standing by the Soviets.
KGB agents, however, apprehended anyone who tried to come
near it. Now it is again the symbol of independent Latvia, and
locals lay flowers between the two soldiers who stand guard at
the monument base.

▲▲**St. Peter's Church** (Pētera baznīca)—St. Peter's distinctive wooden spire, which used to be the tallest structure in
Riga, burned down during World War II. The present steel
replica was built during the Soviet period. Take the elevator up
to the observation deck for 1 lat (students 70 s). You can visit
the inside of the church afterwards (Tuesday–Sunday 10:00–
20:00, September–April 10:00–17:00, closed Monday, in the
Old Town).

▲▲**Riga Dom** (Doma baznīca)—Also in the Old Town, Riga's most formidable church dates from 1211. You can go inside for 30 s (Tuesday–Friday 13:00–17:00, Saturday 10:00–14:00, closed Monday). The inscriptions recall Latvia's German Lutheran heritage, and in fact the crypt holds what's left of Bishop Albert of Bremen, who started it all. The Dom has a first-class organ and often hosts good choirs; concert tickets (usually under 3 Ls) are available at the ticket office at Riharda Vāgnera iela 4 or downstairs in the Filharmonic building at Amatu iela 6 (both a few blocks away and open daily 12:00–15:00 and 16:00–19:00). Just down the street from the Dom toward the river is a statue of the philosopher Johann Gottfried Herder, born in Riga in 1744, whose influential writings on nationalism were shaped partly by growing up among the Balts.

▲▲**Museum of the History of Riga and Navigation** (Rīgas vēstures un kugniecības muzejs)—Although there are only a few English labels, this museum gives a good idea of Riga's early history on the Baltic–Black Sea trade route, explains the Old Town's street plan in terms of a now-silted-up river that used to flow through the center, and highlights inter-war Riga. History buffs will want to spend several hours exploring (1 Ls, students 40 s, Wednesday–Sunday 11:00–17:00, closed Monday and Tuesday, Palasta iela 4, behind the Dom).

▲▲**Central Market** (Centrālais tirgus)—This is the most accessible and thriving central market in all of the Baltics and gives you a real insight into life here. It sprawls in and around the large former Zeppelin hangars between the train station and the river (go under the tracks).

▲▲**Other Attractions**—If you have more time, check out the **Museum of Decorative Arts** (Dekoratīvi lietikās mākslas muzejs) at Skārņu iela 10/20; the **Motor Museum** (Motor-muzejs) on S. Eizenšteina iela in suburban Riga, which houses the cars of Soviet leaders, including Stalin's (take bus #21 along Brīvības iela); or even farther out, in good weather, the **Open-Air Ethnographic Museum** (Etnogrāfiskais brīvdabas muzejs), which shows farm buildings from all over Latvia (take bus #1 along Brīvības iela to the first stop across the bridge over Lake Jugla).

Sleeping in Riga
(.6 lats = about $1)
If you're calling from the U.S.A., dial 011-371, then the local

number; for more phone info, see the Appendix: Dialing Direct Within Russia & the Baltics.

Hotels

Radi un Draugi is an excellent small hotel right in the Old Town with modern renovated rooms and bathrooms (singles with bath 23.60 Ls, doubles 29.50 Ls, breakfast not included, reserve ahead, Mārstaļu iela 1, LV-1050 Riga, tel. 722-0372, fax 724-2239).

Hotel Laine is small, clean, and downtown. With shared bath, singles cost 14 Ls, doubles 19 Ls, and triples 26 Ls. Doubles with private baths cost 31 to 39 Ls. Breakfast is included. You can walk from the stations or the Old Town, or you can cross the street from the train station and take trolleybus #3 from the stop on Merķeļa iela for two stops; this will leave you on Kr. Valdemāra iela around the block from the hotel. At Skolas iela 11, look for the "Laine" sign, go into the courtyard, in the door on the far left, and up to the reception on the third floor (zip code: LV1010, tel. 728-8816, fax 728-7658).

The Riga **tourist information office** rents three nice rooms with two hall bathrooms right above its office in the Old Town. One is $30, another $40, and the third goes for $50 (Skārņu iela 22, tel. 722-1731, fax 722-7680).

Valdemār Hotel indeed used to be a hotel for Supreme Soviet deputies. It hasn't been remodeled—the bathrooms need a little work and the furniture is very old—and one has the feeling that the members are staying elsewhere now. Still, it's in a beautiful Art Nouveau building, and retains some order, civility, and shabby dignity, so it's an option if other places are full. Sweaty backpackers will feel underdressed and should stay elsewhere. Walk from the station or follow the same directions as for Hotel Laine, above. Doubles with bath cost 28 Ls, singles 18 Ls (Kr. Valdemāra iela 23, LV1010, catty-corner from the State Museum of Latvian Art, tel. 733-2132 or 733-4462, fax 733-3001).

Hotel Viktorija's renovated doubles with bath are also an option, though at 34 Ls they are more expensive than other more convenient hotels. Avoid the unrenovated rooms for 10 Ls (A. Čaka iela 55, LV 1011, tel. 2/272-305, fax 2/276-209). From the train station, the hotel is 8 walkable blocks up Marijas iela (which turns into A Čaka iela); you can also hop on trolleybus #11, #18, or #23. The Alus Krogs (beer hall)

Staburags on the ground floor of the Viktorija building is in the same traditional Latvian style as the Alus Sēta on Dome Square, and a good place for sauerkraut soup or a pint of Aldaris beer.

Hostelers should try to get into the **University of Latvia dormitory**, in the Old Town about five minutes' walk from the train station (Basteja bulvāris 10, LV 1050, tel. 721-6221). Assorted singles and doubles with hall showers and toilets cost 2 Ls to 7 Ls per room. Respectable quarters; unbeatable location; try to call ahead. It's above the Europcar office; a sign outside also says "Latvijas Universitate Studentu Kopmītnes." Fewer rooms are available in winter.

Private Rooms

Patricija Ltd. speaks English and finds rooms with families in Riga for an average of $15 per person per night without breakfast. Entire apartments (minimum three nights' stay) cost $40 to $60 per night. They also do sightseeing tours and provide guides. Call ahead or stop by their office (Monday–Friday 9:00–18:00, Saturday and Sunday 10:00–13:00, very near the train station, Elizabetes iela 22, apartment 6, on the third floor up a dark stairway, tel. 728-4868, tel. & fax 728-6650).

Host Family Association also arranges homestays in Riga ($30 for one person, $50 for two, tel. & fax 7/812/275-1992 in St. Petersburg, e-mail: hofak.hop.stu.neva.ru).

Eating in Riga

Rozamunde features a pre-WWII Latvian ambience and menu, such as chicken stuffed with dried fruit for 4.10 Ls. The upstairs Hercog Jekab room, dedicated to this Latvian hero, has a 19th-century menu and decor (11:00–02:30, live music nightly—singing or harp, Mazā Smilšu 8, tel. 722-7798). The same owner runs **Vērdiņš**, a French creperie and restaurant in the Old Town, with tasteful indoor/outdoor seating and moderate prices (daily 10:00–23:00, crepes 1–2.50 Ls, entrées around 3.50 Ls, Mazā Pils iela 11).

Near the Dome Square, **Alus sēta** at Tirgoņu iela 6 is a beer hall and restaurant in traditional Latvian style with self-service from the grill (daily 11:00–01:00, bean soup 80 s, pork kebab 1.70 Ls, Latvian-style peas with bacon 80 s).

Put Vējini at Jauniela 18/22 has a restaurant upstairs (entrées about 3.50–9 Ls) and a bar with a fireplace downstairs (daily 12:00–23:00). In summer you can down a beer (Aldaris is Latvia's most popular brand) at the outdoor cafés in the square.

Fredis Café serves small, tasty, sub sandwiches in the Old Town (0.80–1.30 Ls, halves possible). Seating is limited; call ahead for large take-out orders. Vegetarian options and English menus are available (daily 9:00–24:00, Audēju iela 5, tel. 721-3731).

Lido has good, cheap Latvian food, such as stuffed cabbage with mushroom sauce for 1.75 Ls (take-out or sit down, Elizabetes iela 65, near State Museum of Lativan Art).

Pizza Lulu bakes big whole pizzas for 5 Ls to 6.50 Ls and serves slices for 69 s to 85 s. Try the Suino (daily 8:00–24:00, Gērtrudes iela 27, near Tērbatas, for delivery call 2/361-234).

At **Rama**, cheap and filling Indian vegetarian food is dished out by, you guessed it, the International Society for Krishna Consciousness (all profits go to charity). They don't try to convert foreigners, and whatever you think of their beliefs, they do get credit for feeding a lot of hungry, impoverished Latvians and providing a place to recover from a week of fried cutlets. It's a fascinating sociological experience to see so many Eastern Europeans in face paint and saris, and where else but Riga can you eat with the Hare Krishnas without being afraid your friends will see you? (Monday–Saturday 8:00–20:30, Sunday 11:00–18:00, Kr. Barona iela 56, the café is through the front door and to the left).

Osiris, which shares an entrance with the Aperto Libro bookstore, is the kind of place to pick up a croissant and orange juice in the morning, and fine for lunch or dinner too. They have foreign newspapers on the tables and entrées for 2.50 Ls to 3 Ls (Monday–Friday 8:00–24:00, Saturday–Sunday 10:00–24:00, Kr. Barona iela 31).

For **picnic fixings**, go to the Central Market behind the train station (see Sights, above). Most neighborhoods have small 24-hour grocery stores, and a Universal Veikals supermarket should open soon (1 block off Aspazijas in central Riga).

Near Riga: Jūrmala

A sunny summer day might be the time to go to **Jūrmala**, Riga's seaside resort. You can't swim (too polluted), but you can set up a beach chair. Go to the local-trains departure hall in the station; trains to Jūrmala are posted in red. Tickets to Majori, the most popular section of Jūrmala, are available from the windows in the same hall. Other popular short trips are to towns such as Sigulda, Cēsis, and Valmiera along the Gauja River northeast of Riga.

Transportation Connections—Riga

By Train

Riga's train station (*centrālā stacija*), though not overly crowded, is confusing at first. Take a look at the Riga city map at the beginning of the chapter. The long-distance train departure hall is #4 on our map. To one side of it are ticket windows 3 through 9; to the other side is the entrance to the tunnel to the platforms.

The local-train departure hall is #3 on our city map. In its near right corner is a passage leading to hall #2 and windows 25 through 34.

For tickets to Moscow, St. Petersburg, and Vilnius, and other long-distance trains running on the territory of the former Soviet Union, you need to visit either windows 3 through 8 in hall #4 or windows 25 through 30 in hall #2. Your nationality doesn't matter, and it doesn't matter whether you are buying same-day or advance tickets.

For tickets on the Baltic Express to Tallinn and Warsaw, and generally on long-distance trains which are not part of the

Trains Departing Riga

#	To	Leaves	Arrives	2nd Class	1st Class
2	Moscow (Maskava)	17:40	11:00	23 Ls	47 Ls
4	"	18:50	12:20	"	"
38	St. Petersburg (S-Pēterburga)	19:25	8:37	20 Ls	39 Ls
221	Vilnius (Viļņa)	23:45	7:13	6 Ls	10 Ls
8	Tallinn	5:20	11:55	7 Ls	14 Ls
7	Warsaw (via *Šeštokai*)	0:25	13:12	19 Ls	28 Ls

old Soviet "Express" ticketing system, you need to go to an office at Turgeņeva iela 14, 2 blocks from the train station at the corner of Timoteja iela (look for the "Dzelceļa kases" sign, Monday–Saturday 8:00–19:00, Sunday 8:00–18:00). After this office closes for the evening, window 9 at the station (in hall #4) can help you with tickets on these trains.

Train #2, the *Latvijas Ekspresis* to Moscow, is Latvia's flagship. On board, conductors provide newspapers, serve meals in your compartment, and are rumored to speak English.

Trains #7 and #8 are the Estonian-run Baltic Express, which you pick up in Riga on its way between Tallinn and Warsaw (with a change of trains at Šeštokai, Lithuania). The overnight train to Tallinn has been discontinued and since taking the Baltic Express just to Tallinn is a little more expensive (and the timing is awkward), you should go by bus.

By Bus

The bus is the best way from Riga to Tallinn or Vilnius. Coming from the train station, Riga's bus station (*autoosta*) is on the other side of the tracks, then two minutes' walk past the central market towards the river. Buy tickets from windows 2 through 8 in the main hall. Look for the information window (#1); they charge 2 santims for questions, and 4 santims for "complicated" questions.

Try to take a bus that makes as few stops as possible en route. The buses which run from Tallinn to Vilnius via Riga (starred below) are the fastest, nonstop, and very comfortable. Be wary of the 8:10 to Vilnius, which terminates in Minsk.

Riga to Tallinn: In summer 1997 buses to Tallinn left from platform 1 at 3:05, 6:35*, 7:20, 11:50, 13:00*, 17:10, and 03:30, arriving at 8:20, 12:05, 13:20, 17:50, 18:00, 00:10, and 9:45, respectively. The fare was 6 Ls.

Riga to Vilnius: Buses to Vilnius left from platform 2 at 8:10, 11:00, 17:40*, 0:20, 2:00, and 3:45*, arriving five to six hours later. Tickets cost 6 Ls.

Riga to Warsaw: There's a daily overnight bus to Warsaw leaving at 18:00 from platform 1 (tickets 14 Ls).

By Boat

The ferry port in Riga is a little north of the Old Town. You can walk, but it's easier to catch a cab, or to take tram 5 or 9 to the Jūrskola stop. Passenger ferry service runs twice a week to

Travemünde in Germany and three times a week to Slite, Gotland in Sweden. Check the latest edition of *Riga In Your Pocket.*

By Air
Connections between the Airport and Downtown: Riga's airport (*lidosta*) has been remodeled into adequate working order. If you take a taxi from (or to) the airport you will be ripped off. Instead, buy a 14-s bus ticket and board bus #22, which runs between the airport and Arhitektu iela 13 in the center of town.

For booking and reconfirmation: In the city, you can get tickets for most airlines at the Lufthansa City Center (Monday–Friday 9:00–18:00, Saturday 10:00–14:00, Kr. Barona iela 7/9, tel. 728-5901 or 728-5614, fax 782-8199).

VILNIUS, LITHUANIA

Sprawling and disorganized, a Catholic church on every corner, Vilnius is the homiest and coziest of the three Baltic capitals, and also the most unsophisticated and run-down. A restful, horizontal city, Vilnius' one- and two-story buildings and its arches and courtyards are more reminiscent of a friendly Polish provincial capital than of the tall German-influenced architecture in Riga or the Hanseatic frosting-cake feel of Tallinn. No wonder, considering Lithuania's centuries-long political and religious ties with Poland, and the fact that Poland occupied Vilnius from 1920 to 1939 while most of the rest of Lithuania was independent.

Vilnius' Old Town (the buildings date largely from the 17th and 18th centuries) is huge and, unlike Riga's or Tallinn's, amazingly dilapidated. Burned-out windows, crumbling wooden shutters, cracked plaster, and bowed roofs cry out for millions of dollars' worth of restoration work (while certain Soviet "improvements," like the central telephone office, cry out for the wrecking ball). The fact that Vilnius is falling apart gives the visitor a heightened sense of possibility. Every paneless window and paintless shutter makes you think of what could be there: a family, a shop, candles on the table, children playing on the floor. Riga and Tallinn, in contrast, are much more accounted for.

Vilnius' disorganization also challenges you to explore. The Old Town is full of cozy cafés and fascinating galleries and shops, but you have to duck through archways into courtyards, open gates and doors, and slowly learn your way from nook to cranny. Some streets, such as Stikliỹ, transport you back to turn-of-the-century Eastern Europe, when Vilnius was an ethnic hodgepodge of Lithuanians, Poles, White Russians, and a booming Jewish community. These days Vilnius is half Lithuanian, half Polish and Russian, and all three languages are very much in evidence on the streets. Lithuania as a whole, however, is 80 percent Lithuanian and less than 10 percent Russian. Russian minority rights are not as big an issue here.

Paradoxically, while Lithuania is the Baltic state with the smallest Slavic population, it is the most Slavic in temperament and feel. Vilnius, as the only inland Baltic capital, was always politically and economically closer to Poland and Russia than to Scandinavia. Lithuania has a government of former Gorbachev-era reform Communists. Lithuanian politics and society have the mildly theatrical quality that you see in Russia but not in Latvia or Estonia. And Vilnius certainly feels like more of a Soviet city than Tallinn—though this is not the harsh, urban Sovietism of Riga, but rather the provincial inertia that at the same time makes Vilnius endearing.

Planning Your Time
Vilnius merits a two-day stay.

Day 1
11:00 Hike up Castle Hill and climb the tower.
13:00 Walk down Gedimino prospektas and lunch at Prie arlamento.
14:00 Visit the Jewish Museum.
15:00 Wander through the Old Town and look into its churches, shops, and university.
18:00 Take a taxi out to dinner at Ritos smuklė.

Day 2
10:00 Visit the KGB Museum.
12:00 Lunch at Ritos Slėptuvė.
14:00 Check out the two branches of the National Museum.
18:00 End your visit with dinner at the Hotel Naujasis ilnius.

Orientation
Vilnius' Old Town sprawls from the river and the cathedral all the way up to the train station. Walking from the station

Vilnius

downhill to the river is pleasant. To reach the Old Town from the bus and train stations, turn right out the front door of the train station and follow Geležinkelio gatvė down the hill along the train tracks, then turn left down Aušros Vartų gatvė where the tracks cross on an overpass. Go straight through the Auéros Vartai (Gates of Dawn) and keep heading downhill.

Tourist Information: The comprehensive tourist office offers lots of info, maps, and walking tours (Monday–Friday 9:00–18:00, Saturday 10:00–15:00, Gedimino prospektas 14, tel. 616-867, fax 226-118). An incredibly good city guidebooklet called *Vilnius In Your Pocket* is on sale everywhere in town for 4 litas (Lt). As soon as you arrive and change money, go to the nearest kiosk and buy it for its wit, trolleybus map, and feature stories. This book can't possibly hope to better the complete information in *VIYP*. We have, however, tried to save you having to mow through its masses of detail by selecting the best few restaurants, hotels, and sights. If you exhaust the restaurant or hotel choices that we've listed below, refer to *Vilnius In Your Pocket.*

American Embassy: Akmenu gatvė 6, slightly west of the Old Town, tel. 223-031 or 222-729.

Bookstore: The **Littera** bookstore in the courtyard of the university (enter from Universiteto gatvė) has maps, postcards, Penguins, and books about Lithuania in English (Monday–Thursday 10:00–18:00, Friday 10:00–17:00).

Currency Exchange
4 litas (Lt) = about $1, 1 lita = 100 centas (c)
Booths everywhere have similar rates, including the 24-hour bureau next to the train station. Among others, the Vilniaus Bankas at Gedimino prospektas 10 has an ATM and also changes American Express traveler's checks for a 2 percent commission (exchange window open Monday–Friday 9:00–21:00, Saturday 10:00–21:00, Sunday 10:00–18:00, lunch break 12:30–13:30). The American Express representative is at šeimyniskiŋ gatvė 12 (Monday–Friday 8:00–20:00). The bank in the post office also exchanges traveler's checks. Taupomasis Bankas has ATMs at four of its branches (Vilniaus gatvė 16 is the most convenient).

Telephones and Mail
The main telephone office, open 24 hours daily, is on Vilniaus gatvė 33 (enter from Islandijos gatvė). This is the place to buy a phone card to use in the efficient blue Norwegian phones in this office and in phone booths around town (smallest denomination: 3.54 Lt; tear off the corner before you insert the card). Per minute, calls to Latvia or Estonia cost 1.66 Lt; to Russia, 3.54 Lt; to Europe, 5.79 Lt; and to

the U.S., 10.51 Lt. There are also "call now–pay later" metered booths in the phone office.

The main post office, at Gedimino prospektas 7, has card-operated phones and "talk now–pay later" booths (Monday–Friday 8:00–20:00, Saturday 11:00–17:00).

Getting Around Vilnius

Vilnius has trolleybuses (with overhead wires) and regular buses (without wires). Both trolleybuses and buses use named stops, and people in Vilnius often refer to their location by the name of the nearest bus stop. The trolleybuses are more convenient, because *Vilnius In Your Pocket* includes a handy map listing routes and stop names. Tickets, available from kiosks, cost 60 c apiece.

Taxis around the center should cost about 6 Lt to 10 Lt, 10 Lt to 15 Lt out to the suburbs. To summon an honest cabbie, avoid the private taxi companies and call the efficient central city-run dispatcher at 228-888 (try to find someone who speaks Lithuanian or Russian to help).

Sights—Vilnius

▲▲▲**KGB Prison**—After the KGB withdrew from Vilnius, their former prisoners set up a museum in the building where they were once held and beaten, and started giving tours to anyone who would listen. Many Lithuanians were interned here briefly before being deported to Siberia during the 1940s, and the part of the building you will see—including the cells, the padded isolation/torture chamber, appalling photographs of brutally murdered people, and piles of shredded KGB documents—is formally known as the Museum of Genocide of the People of Lithuania. Ask them for the English translation of the exhibits. The museum is free, but despite these people's years of suffering they have very little budget. Consider dropping a 5-Lt coin in the donation box (Tuesday–Sunday 10:00–16:00 though hours may vary, closed Monday, Gedimino prospektas 40, entrance at Aukų gatvė 4, tel. 622-449).

▲▲**Jewish State Museum**—Its two buildings are a block apart. The **Holocaust Exhibition** is at Pamėnkalnio gatvė 12, in the green house on the hill. Before World War II, 240,000 Jews lived in Lithuania; 95 percent of them perished during the war. Vilnius, which was 30 percent Jewish in 1914, was for many years the intellectual and cultural center of Eastern European Jewry. The exhibit first documents pre-war Jewish life in Vilnius (including blowups of powerful documentary photographs by Roman Vishniac), then its extermination by the Nazis, including one German commandant's chilling daily execution record. Admission is free, but donations are gratefully accepted. The staff will be happy to interpret if they're not busy and can also provide guided tours to Jewish historical sites around Lithuania if you contact them in advance at tel. 620-730 (Monday–Thursday 9:00–17:00, Friday 9:00–16:00, closed weekends).

The newly reopened **Exhibition on Jewish Life** is on the second floor of Pylimo gatvė 4. One room shows relics of the city's Great Synagogue, bombed toward the end of World War II and torn down shortly thereafter. The other room is reserved for changing displays (free, donations accepted, Monday–Thursday 9:00–17:00, Friday 9:00–16:00). Booklets, postcards, and crafts are on sale.

Ask the staff at either museum how to get to Paneriai, outside Vilnius, where the Nazis murdered 100,000 people, 70,000 of them Jews.

▲▲**Castle Hill**—Hike up to the top from the square near the cathedral. If it's a nice day, bring a picnic lunch. Buy a ticket (4 Lt, students 2 Lt, free on Wednesday) and climb up to the roof of **Gedimino Tower**, at the top of the hill, to see Vilnius spread out before you (and in the distance, to the west, the TV tower where Soviet troops killed 14 unarmed Lithuanians in January 1991). Gedimino Tower (daily 11:00–18:00) also houses a small museum.

▲**Lithuanian National Museum** (Lietuvos Nacionalinis Muziejus)—The second-floor exhibition on inter-war independent Lithuania is the most colorful and thus probably the most interesting to non-Lithuanian speakers (4 Lt, students 2 Lt, Wednesday–Sunday 11:00–18:00, October–April 11:00–17:00, closed Monday and Tuesday, Arsenalo gatvė 1, in the long, low building at the northwest base of Castle Hill).

The National Museum's exhibit on Lithuania from 1940 to 1991 is housed separately in a large, white, Soviet-modern building along the north riverbank (past the multistory Hotel Lietuva). Though it's entirely in Lithuanian and Russian, the displays on the deportation and the independence struggle are very moving. Check out the tree trunk where Lithuanians nailed their discarded Soviet medals and pins in 1991 (4 Lt, students 2 Lt, free Wednesday, Tuesday–Sunday 12:00–18:00, October–April 12:00–17:00, closed Monday).

▲**Churches**—Consider visiting the **Vilnius Cathedral** (Vilniaus Katedra), whose walls and pillars are hung with dozens of religious paintings (you might see a wedding too); **St. John's Church** (Šv. Jono) at Pilies gatvė and Šv. Jono gatvė; and the **Gates of Dawn** (Aušros Vartai) on Aušros Vartų gatvė (be sure to walk up the long hallway and the stairs to the chapel in the archway over the street).

▲**Trakai**—This picture-perfect castle is an hour from Vilnius, on an island in the middle of a lake. Buses leave frequently from the Vilnius bus station.

Sleeping in Vilnius
(4 Lt = about $1)

If you're calling from the U.S.A., dial 011-370-2, then the local number; for more phone info, see the Appendix: Dialing Direct Within Russia & the Baltics.

Hotels

The going rate for a room within walking distance of the Old Town is around 250 Lt to 300 Lt ($60–75) for a double with bath. Prepare for a functional but dated bathroom with Soviet-era tiling and plumbing, or spend a little bit more money for complete modern Western comforts.

Hotel Naujasis Vilnius is a big hotel just across the river from the Old Town with an excellent restaurant, remodeled rooms, and quite acceptable unremodeled rooms. With private bath, TV, and telephone, unremodeled singles cost 180 Lt to 200 Lt, doubles 230 Lt to 250 Lt; remodeled singles are 290 Lt, doubles 330 Lt. Breakfast is included and Visa, Master-Card, and Amex are accepted (Ukmergės gatvė 14, 2600 Vilnius, tel. 721-342, fax 723-161).

Hotel Vilniaus Narutis, in a newly renovated 16th-century building, offers comfortable rooms, a restaurant, courtyard, sauna, gym equipment, and a central location in the Old Town. With private bath and breakfast, singles are 200 Lt to 240 Lt, doubles 220 Lt to 480 Lt; all credit cards are accepted (room service, laundry, Pilies 24, 2000 Vilnius, tel. 610-981, fax 223-962).

Hotel Pilaitė is a ten-room hotel near the Naujasis Vilnius, in the building with the tower on the right just across the bridge from the Old Town. The reception is on the second floor. It's central and friendly with pleasant rooms and a great breakfast. Reservations are recommended (with bath, singles are 240 Lt, doubles 280 Lt, suites 316 Lt, breakfast served in room, Kalvarijų gatvė 1, 2600 Vilnius, tel. 752-292, fax 752-269).

Hotel Victoria is an attractively priced Swedish-managed hotel. It has double rooms with bath for only 240 Lt—unfortunately it's not within walking distance of the main tourist sites, but you may be able to manage if you have a car or like taking buses and taxis (Saltoniškių gatvė 56, 2600 Vilnius, tel. 724-013, fax 724-320, e-mail: victoria@tdd.lt).

Hotel Neringas is an acceptable, clean, fairly modern hotel with a comfortable carpeted lobby. It's central but feels a little overpriced. With breakfast and private bath, singles are 300 Lt, and doubles are 380 Lt. Reception is on the second floor (Gedimino prospektas 23, 2001 Vilnius, reserve ahead, tel. 610-516, fax 614-160).

Zaliasis Tiltas (Green Bridge) is an old, run-down but tolerable, and very central Soviet-era hotel with a depressing lobby and a friendly staff who speak some English. It's not a first choice, but perhaps a fallback. With TV, breakfast, and private bath, singles are 90 Lt to 250 Lt and doubles are 130 Lt to 320 Lt (credit cards accepted, Gedimino prospektas 12, 2001 Vilnius, tel. 615-450, fax 221-716).

Private Rooms

Litinterp can house you with a family in the Old Town for 60 Lt to 100 Lt for a single or 140 Lt for a double, breakfast included (Monday–Friday 9:00–18:00, Saturday 9:00–16:00, Sunday closed, Bernardinų gatvė 7-2, 2001 Vilnius, tel. 223-291 or 223-850, fax 223-559, e-mail: litinterp@omnitel.net). Also ask them about airport pickup (50 Lt), translators (350 Lt per ten-hour day), long-term apartment rentals, and car rental (260 Lt per day with unlimited mileage for a Renault 21, credit cards accepted).

Host Family Association also arranges homestays in Vilnius ($30 for one person, $50 for two, tel. & fax 7/812/275-1992 in St. Petersburg, e-mail: alexei@hofak.hop.stu.neva.ru).

Hostels ... and the Train Station

The **Lithuanian youth hostel** (Lietuvos Jaunimo Nakvynės Namai) has 52 beds in two- to eight-bed rooms and charges 28 Lt per person Filaretų gatvė 17, 2007 Vilnius, tel. 696-627, fax 220-149 or 262-660, e-mail: filareta@ljtc.vno.osf.lt).

Take bus #34 from outside the train station and to the right (opposite McDonald's) to the seventh stop: "Filaretų." During business hours you can stop by their main office within easy walking distance of the train station. Head left out of the train station and down Šopeno gatvė, which turns into Kauno gatvė (Monday–Friday 8:00–18:30, Kauno gatvė 1a, room 407, tel. 262-660, fax 260-631).

Jaunųjų Turistų Centras has ten clean rooms (triples and quads) and few guests. The friendly older women who run this hostel speak Lithuanian and Russian (dorm bed-20 Lt; includes sheets, sporadic hot water, and use of kitchen; Polocko gatvė 7, tel. 613-576, fax 627-742).

In the Vilnius **train station**, you can sleep cheap in a carriage equipped with lights and clean linen. Through the main arrival/departure hall, look for the sign *Budinti* (36 beds, 15 Lt per person, mandatory "wake up-get out" call at 8:00, Gelžinkelio gatvė 16, tel. 692-472).

Eating in Vilnius

Lithuania is large enough to have a few truly distinctive culinary concoctions. If you get the chance, try *cepeliniai* (literally "zeppelins"—monstrous potato dumplings filled with meat— enough for two people) or *éakotis* (a 2-foot-high, spiky cylindrical cake sometimes sold by the layer at cafés).

Ritos Slėptuvė (Rita's Hideout) is along the south bank of the river not far from the KGB prison museum. Chicago meets Vilnius. This dark basement hangout is run by Rita Dapkutė, a Lithuanian-American who was the director of the Lithuanian Parliament's Information Bureau during the independence struggle. The menu features spaghetti for 6 Lt to 8 Lt and large pizzas for 30 Lt to 50 Lt. Great burgers, too, but avoid the vegetables with rice (Monday–Thursday 7:30– 02:00, Friday–Saturday 7:30–04:00, credit cards accepted Goštauto gatvė 8). You can also order pizza delivery from Rita's at tel. 620-589.

Ritos Smuklė (Rita's Tavern) is as Lithuanian as Ritos Slėptuvė is American. This is the place to get all those Lithuanian specialities you've been hearing about, in a dining room mocked up to look like a country kitchen. Two huge meat *cepeliniai* will cost you 7 Lt, and you can also get tongue, beet borscht, cabbage soup, and *blyniai* (pancakes). You can get there by cab (about 10–12 Lt from the Old Town) or by trolleys 9, 12,

13, or 17—get off in front of the Iki supermarket and do your shopping after you eat (credit cards accepted, Žirmūnų gatvė 68).

At the **Hotel Naujasis Vilnius**, against all odds, a ground-floor dining room in a vast concrete Soviet-style hotel has been transformed into a warm and friendly place to have dinner. Those who've stayed in similar but unreformed provincial hotels in Russia may weep at the sight of this place. The menu is posted at the door, the waiters speak English and smile, candles shine on every table in the winter, and artfully prepared entrées from a wide-ranging menu average 25 Lt (daily 7:30–22:30; Visa, MasterCard, and Amex accepted; Ukmergės gatvė 14, in the hotel).

Prie Parlamento is indeed right by Parliament but not as fancy as its name suggests—it serves three meals a day at low prices from a big English-language menu. This is the place to linger over a big breakfast with friends and a newspaper (Monday–Thursday 8:00–02:00, Friday 8:00–16:00, Saturday–Sunday 10:00–02:00, Gedimino prospektas 46).

Prie Universiteto, a comfy bar/restaurant in the Old Town, is a good place for late-night food (daily 10:30–02:00, Dominikonų gatvė 9).

Trys Draugai serves steaks and Hungarian food right where all the amber and souvenir sellers congregate. It's a little expensive for Vilnius but very popular with tourists (daily 12:00–24:00, Pilies gatvė 25a).

Vilnius has a fleet of Western-style **supermarkets** including five outlets of the home-grown **Iki** chain. The only Iki within any sort of walking distance of downtown is near Parliament at Jasinskio gatvė 16 (Jasinskio is the continuation of Pamėnkalnio and number 16 is on your left just before crossing the river, Monday–Saturday 9:00–21:00, Sunday 9:00–18:00).

Transportation Connections—Vilnius

By Train
All long-haul ticket sales are now in the large hall to the right as you enter the train station (Geležinkelio stotis). Windows 5 through 7 sell tickets to destinations in the former Soviet Union (daily 8:00–19:30) and windows 3 and 4 sell international tickets. The windows straight ahead as you enter the station (8 through 14) are for domestic tickets only.

If you want to purchase a sleeper berth on an overnight

Trains Departing Vilnius

#	To	Leaves	Arrives	2nd Class	1st Class
6	Moscow (Maskva)	16:48	9:12	80 Lt	135 Lt
26	St. Petersburg (Sankt Peterburgas)	21:32*	11:30	65 Lt	102 Lt
221	Riga (Ryga)	23:30	655	44 Lt	65 Lt

*On even days, another train departs at 19:10.

train (say to St. Petersburg), you might be told to return three hours before the train arrives (when they know the availability of births); at that time you can purchase a birth though a specific compartment won't be assigned until you board the train.

By Bus
The Vilnius bus station is across the street from the train station. Look for the *Autobusų stotis* sign. The ticket windows are in the right half of the building. Windows 11–12, around the corner to the right as you enter, sell tickets to all destinations outside Lithuania. There's no problem getting seats on buses although it is sensible to come a few hours in advance in case there are last-minute lines.

Vilnius to Tallinn: Buses leave daily at 8:00 and 21:45, arriving at 18:00 and 8:20; tickets cost 81 Lt.

Vilnius to Riga: Departures are at 8:00, 12:40, 17:10, 19:30, 21:45, and 0:30, arriving five to six hours later for 40 Lt.

Vilnius to Warsaw: Buses leave at 10:00, 19:30, 20:30, and 21:30 daily, arriving in Warsaw about ten hours later for 65 Lt. The 10:00 bus runs to Warszawa Zachodnia station, the 19:30 to Warszawa Wschodnia, and the 20:30 and 21:30 buses stop at both stations.

By Air
Instead of tearing down the old Stalin-era terminal at Vilnius's airport, or building a new one on a different side of the runway, they piggybacked a new terminal on top of the old one. It's a unique creation.

Connections between the Airport and Downtown:
Reach the airport on bus #2 (not trolleybus #2), direction:
"Aerouostas." It stops on the same side of Ukmergės gatvė as
the Hotel Lietuva, then several times in the Old Town. All you
need is a regular 60-c bus ticket. Taxis from the airport will try
to rip you off.

For booking and reconfirmation: You can buy tickets at
the airport; at the Lufthansa City Center on Gedimino
prospektas 37 (Monday–Friday 9:00–18:00, Saturday
9:00–14:00, tel. 223-147), or at Baltic Travel Service in the Old
Town (Subačiaus gatvė 2, tel. 220 151).

Near Vilnius: Kaunas

Kaunas was Lithuania's capital between the wars when Vilnius
was occupied by Poland. It's cozier and more walkable than
Vilnius. Since it's 80 percent Lithuanian versus Vilnius' 50 percent, some claim Kaunas is the "real Lithuania."

Kaunas is an easy day trip from Vilnius. Minibuses
(*mikroautobusai*) to Kaunas leave roughly on the hour from the
Vilnius bus station (platform 37, 9 Lt). The trip takes about 90
minutes. Regular-size buses run to Kaunas every half-hour, but
take two hours. The train also takes about two hours. The
Kaunas bus and train stations are only a block away from each
other but more than a mile from the Old Town.

When you arrive in Kaunas, buy a copy of *Kaunas In Your
Pocket* (if you didn't get one at the bus station in Vilnius), then
hop into a taxi and ask to be taken to the Rotušės aikštė: **Town
Hall square**. This should cost about 5 Lt to 7 Lt and leave you
at the central square of Kaunas's Old Town. From here, you
can first explore the Old Town and then walk the approximately 2 kilometers back to the station along Kaunas' grand
pedestrian street, called first Vilniaus gatvė and then Laisvės
aleja. There are plenty of small cafés along these streets.

One block to the left (north) of Laisvės aleja is Donelaičio
gatvė, where you'll find the drab **Military Museum** of Vytautas
the Great (Vytauto Didziojo Karo Muziejus), which preserves
the airplane in which two Lithuanian-American aviators crashed
while trying to make a nonstop New York–Kaunas flight in
1933. Behind this is the **Art Museum** (Dailės Muziejus) in
whose newer wing you can listen to music by the Lithuanian
composer M. K. Čiurlionis (1875–1911) and then look at paintings in which he tried to present the same structures visually.

Kaunas

(Vytautas Landsbergis, the former Lithuanian president, first made his reputation as a Čiurlionis scholar.) The **Devil's Museum** (Velnių Muziejus), across the street at Putvinskio gatvė 64, is a collection of hundreds of folk-art devil carvings; the well-known one of Hitler and Stalin divvying up Lithuania is on the second floor. All these museums are open Tuesday through Sunday only (closed Monday and the last Tuesday of each month).

With more time, see **Ninth Fort** (a Nazi internment camp) or beautiful **Pazaislis monastery**, just outside Kaunas.

Sleeping in Kaunas
(4 Lt = about $1)
The city code for Kaunas is 7. If you're calling from the U.S.A., dial 011-370-7 before the local number; from elsewhere in Lithuania, dial 8-27 first.

Hotel Lietuva at Daukanto gatvė 21 dates from the Soviet era but it is adequately central, clean, and reasonably priced: singles with bath cost 160 Lt, doubles with bath 240–270 Lt, with breakfast, credit cards accepted (tel. 205-992). There are several nice small hotels with $100 doubles in the Old Town; check *Kaunas In Your Pocket*. **Lithuanian Youth Hostels,** at Prancūzų gatvė 59 not far from the stations, offers big rooms with kitchens, bath, and balconies. Members pay 40 Lt for a single or 24 Lt per person in triples; non-members pay 2.5 times more (tel. 748-972, fax 202-761).

TAKING THE TRANS-SIBERIAN RAILWAY EASTWARD

Until recently the Intourist monopoly on eastbound Trans-Siberian tickets meant that travelers in the know took the Trans-Siberian westbound, from Beijing to Moscow. Now the situation has changed, and it is arguably cheaper and easier to get tickets from Moscow to Beijing. We've met many travelers in Moscow who are on their way to Asia by rail.

Highlights of the journey include: the obelisk in the Ural Mountains marking the border between Asia and Europe, picturesque Lake Baikal, impressive border gates between Russia and China, changing of the wheels to a different gauge, and beautiful Manchuria.

Schedule

There are two trains per week to Beijing: a Russian train and a Chinese train. The Russian #20 train leaves Moscow on Friday evening at 20:15, and arrives at 6:32 the following Friday morning in Beijing, a journey of a little over six days. The Chinese #4 train leaves Moscow on Tuesday evenings at 19:53 and arrives in Beijing at 15:33 the following Monday afternoon, a journey of just over 5.5 days. During the summer there is sometimes an extra Russian departure on Saturday evenings. The train station for all departures to China is Yaroslavskii Vokzal (Ярославский Вокзал) at Metro: Komsomolskaya/ Комсомольская. It's the white Art Nouveau station to the right of the Metro building, and the long-distance platforms are on the far side. Arrive at the station an hour before departure.

Routes

Chinese #4 trains from Moscow and Beijing turn south through Mongolia just after they pass Lake Baikal. This route is known as the Trans-Mongolian. Russian #20 trains go around Mongolia to the east, crossing the Russian–Chinese border at Zabaikalsk/Manzhouli and passing through the Chinese city of Harbin. This route is called the Trans-Manchurian. The only train that truly measures up to the name "Trans-Siberian" is the seven-day trip between Moscow and Vladivostok in Russia's Far East. Regardless of your route, consider breaking up your journey with a stop or two (for instance, in Irkutsk and Lake Baikal).

Visas

You will need a Chinese visa, and if you take the Trans-Mongolian, a Mongolian transit visa as well. Most Chinese consulates issue tourist visas with a minimum of hassle. An exception is the consular office in Moscow (Monday, Wednesday, Friday 9:00–12:00, ul. Druzhby/Дружбы 6, Metro: Universitet/Университет, tel. 143-1543). They will issue tourist visas only if you show them your ticket to China and your onward ticket from China, or failing that, a "letter of introduction" from your country's embassy. It is better to get your Chinese visa in another country.

Moscow is, however, an excellent place to get your Mongolian transit visa. The Mongolian consular office is at Spasopesovskii/Спасопесовский per. 7/1 (tel. 244-7867), just steps from the Smolenskaya/Смоленская stop on the dark blue Metro line. From the Metro exit, go straight through the passage under the modern building, turn right (east) down a small street, and walk 1 block to a park with a church on the south side and the American ambassador's residence on the east side. The Mongolian complex is on the northwest—look for the pictures of the camels. The consular entrance is through a marked door near the corner of the building (Monday–Friday, 9:00–13:00). Make sure you already have your Chinese visa to show them, and bring your train ticket too if you have it. You should be able to pick up your completed visa that afternoon or the next day for about $30. Tourist (as opposed to transit) visas to Mongolia, like those to Russia, still require an official invitation.

The Chinese Train vs. the Russian Train

Travelers on the Chinese train require a $30 Mongolian transit visa, but this is easy to get in Moscow. The Russian train takes about half a day longer than the Chinese train, which can be seen as either an advantage or a disadvantage. The scenery on the two routes is comparable.

The main difference between the two trains is inside the cars. It's worth the extra money to go first class. Traveling in the Chinese train's first-class, two-person compartments can be a real pleasure. Each compartment has a table, an armchair, and a washroom (including a shower head and occasionally

Trans-Siberian Timetable:
Moscow to Beijing

The Chinese Train

Day	Time	Station
Tues	19:53	Moscow
Wed	18:15	Perm
Thur	21:11	Novosibirsk
Fri	9:57	Krasnoyarsk
Sat	4:04	Irkutsk
Sun	9:30	Ulaanbaatar
Mon	15:33	Beijing

The Russian Train

Day	Time	Station
Fri	20:15	Moscow
Sat	18:34	Perm
Sun	21:44	Novosibirsk
Mon	10:29	Krasnoyarsk
Tue	4:55	Irkutsk
Thur	12:09	Harbin
Fri	6:32	Beijing

Confirm schedule at station. Note that not all times are local times. For example, the Chinese train arrives in Irkutsk at 8:04 local time, since Irkutsk is 4 hours ahead of Moscow.

lukewarm water) shared with the adjoining compartment. The Russian train's first-class, two-person compartments are nice too, though more plain.

In second class there is less difference. In either case you're in a four-berth compartment of the sort that is great going overnight to St. Petersburg or Tallinn, gets awfully cramped after five days, but can be a lot of fun if you have good company. The Chinese train also has some first-class four-berth compartments, which should be your last choice as they combine the high price of first class with the claustrophobia of having three companions.

The Chinese train has Chinese conductors and furnishings, so you may feel as if you've stepped into China already at the Moscow railway station. During the last two days of a trip on the Russian train, you may feel like you're stuck in a little capsule of Russianness that is persisting into China. This is not true in the restaurant car, which changes at each border.

Bring:

- Dark-colored clothing. (The tracks are rough in spots and you'll likely spill something.) Track suits are comfortable.
- Layered clothing. Compartments have a way of getting too hot and too cold.
- Toilet paper and Kleenex tissues.
- Cup with a handle. If it's big enough, you can use it to "shower."
- Quick-dry washcloth, soap, and Handiwipes for bathing.
- Pocket knife.
- Supply of plastic bags to use for trash and dirty laundry (no laundry facilities aboard).
- Hard-soled thongs for trips to toilet (floor frequently damp).
- Slippers for your cabin.
- Books, handicrafts, CDs, Walkman, extra batteries, and film.
- Best route map you can find, with names of towns in Cyrillic and English. Learn enough Cyrillic (see Appendix) to be able to read the names of towns and menu items.
- Lots of small Russian bills (1,000, 5,000, 10,000, 50,000). No one wants to make change on the train.
- Clean, unwrinkled American dollars in $1, $5, $10, and $20 denominations.
- Two watches (set one for local time and one for Moscow). The timetables that appear on the wall of each car are geared to Moscow time only, and it's helpful to plan ahead for stops at towns along the route. (The train goes through eight time zones.)
- Patience and a good sense of humor.

Food

The food in the restaurant car ranges from good to dismal and is always expensive. The restaurant is open at seemingly arbitrary times, can run out of food, and on the Chinese train, sometimes even disappears between the Russian border and Ulaanbaatar.

Before you go, visit a supermarket in Moscow and load up with enough to feed yourself breakfast plus one meal a day. Some suggestions: bottled water, cartons of juice, bread, cheese, and fruit for the first few days, crisp bread, peanut butter, jelly, tuna fish, chocolate, granola bars, yogurt (the kind that needs no refrigeration), canned food, and fast food–type packets of mustard, mayo, and soy sauce. Also bring instant soup (or ramen noodles), tea, instant coffee, hot chocolate, and anything else that you just add hot water to, as a samovar in each car is kept boiling most of the time. When the train stops (every 3–5 hours), vendors on the platforms sell meat pies, noodles, fruit, veggies, bread, pastries, beer, pop, and bottled water.

Books
Pick up Bryn Thomas's excellent *Trans-Siberian Handbook*, with sights listed by the milepost. Bring a shorter novel than *War and Peace*—on the trip you'll probably be too busy meeting your fellow travelers and buying berries from grandmothers at whistle-stop stations in Siberia to read anything really heavy. A good phrase book and a dictionary (Russian-English and English-Russian) will come in handy.

Buying Tickets for the Trans-Siberian
Buy the biggest compartment you can afford. If you're traveling on the cheap, ask for a top bunk (so you can sleep whenever you want).

From Moscow's Central Railway Agency
If you have friends in Moscow or enough time there yourself, this is the cheapest way to do it. Take the Metro to Komsomolskaya/Комсомольская, go out to the street, find Yaroslavskii Vokzal (the white Art Nouveau station), and then look for the nine-floor, brown apartment building next to it at Krasnoprudnaya/Краснопрудная ul. 1. On the first floor of this building, on the side facing the station, is the branch of the Central Railway Agency where most people buy their Trans-Siberian tickets. You can recognize it by the sign saying Центральное Железнодорожное Агенство in green letters over the door. Head to any of windows 5 through 7. Prepare a piece of paper listing the number of people traveling, your name, nationality, passport number, destination, desired departure date, and desired class. The women at the

ticket counters usually speak Russian only, but will probably understand your request even if it's written in Latin letters.

You don't have to come to the office in person to buy tickets. Someone else can do it for you if they come prepared with the cash and your full name, nationality, and passport number, all of which will be listed on your ticket.

At time of print, prices were as follows: On the Russian train, approximately $165 in a second-class, four-berth compartment and $260 in a first-class, two-berth compartment; on the Chinese train, approximately $157 and $279, respectively. This represents a price *decrease* from past years, and it would not be surprising to see fares rise again.

Demand varies considerably. Tickets to China go on sale at this office 30 days in advance. For most of the year there are no lines at the office, seats are available even just a day in advance, and you'll have your tickets in a matter of minutes. Occasionally though, during summer or during school vacations from mid-January to mid-February, bookings are heavy, lines at the office are not long but move very slowly, and you need to come two or three weeks in advance to get seats, or at least the seats you want. The Chinese trains tend to have more space than the Russian trains, because getting a Mongolian transit visa is a disincentive to many people.

From Travel Agencies

Any travel agency specializing in Russian travel, or any Intourist office abroad, may be able to book Trans-Siberian tickets.

In Moscow: STAR Travel in Moscow charges $217 per person in second class and $322 per person in first class on the Russian train; $257 and $390 on the Chinese train. They may also be able to sell you tickets which allow you to stop in Irkutsk and/or Mongolia along the way. Contact STAR at tel. 974-1781 or 974-1798, fax 280-7686, or e-mail: star@glas.apc.org. STAR is located in the Travellers Guest House (Bolshaya Pereyaslavskaya/Большая Переяславская ulitsa 50, tenth floor). Although STAR normally deals only with youth, it sells Trans-Siberian tickets to travelers of any age.

In St. Petersburg: The St. Petersburg International Hostel can book the Trans-Siberian journey through the hostel's travel agency, **Sindbad Travel** (Monday–Friday 9:30–17:30, tel. 327-8384, fax 329-8019, e-mail: sindbad@ryh.spb.su, hostel's address: 3rd Sovetskaya/3я Советская).

In England: The Russia Experience, which offers various Trans-Siberian tickets, routes, and excursions, also arranges homestays in Russia in conjunction with your journey (Research House, Fraser Road, Perivale, Middlesex UB6 7AQ, England, tel. 0181/566-8846, fax 0181/566-8843, Web site: http://travel.world.co.uk/russiaexp, e-mail: 100604@compuserve.com).

From Finland's Railway Station

If you're in Finland, the international department at the Helsinki train station can write you a Trans-Siberian ticket on the spot, though there are some drawbacks: the markup is high, tickets are sold for the Russian train only, and reconfirmation in Moscow is necessary.

From Monkey Business in Beijing

If you're traveling from Beijing to Moscow, Monkey Business is a convenient, reliable source for Trans-Siberian tickets. They offer an assortment of tickets and packages (though it's cheaper to buy your tickets at the station). A second-class Trans-Siberian trip, including the first night's accommodation in Moscow, costs $340 through Monkey Business. (In contrast, if you buy your ticket at the Beijing train station instead, you'll pay $190 for a second-class ticket; no stopovers or accommodations included.) For an additional $50, Monkey Business processes your Russian visa (Mongolian, too, if needed). They also provide a transfer from their recommended hotels in Beijing to the train station. Do not buy an onward Moscow–Europe train ticket from Monkey Business; these come with substantial markups and are relatively easy to buy in Moscow. (Monkey Business, Beijing Commercial Business Complex, No. 1 Building Yu Lin Li, #406, Youanmenwai, 100054 Beijing, tel. & fax 8610/6329-2244, ext. 4406, e-mail: 100267.2567@compuserve.com).

APPENDIX

Russian Timeline

800s: Spurred by Viking trade along Russia's rivers, states form around the cities of Novgorod and Kiev. ("Russia" comes from a Viking word.)

988: Kiev converts to Christianity and becomes part of the Eastern Orthodox world.

1224–1242: The Mongol hordes invade Russia, conquer, and exact tribute. Russia, however, succeeds where the Baltics failed—at keeping the Germans out.

1465–1557: The Russian czars consolidate power in Moscow, drive away the Mongols, and form a unified Russian state.

1613: Foundation of the Romanov dynasty, which lasts until 1917.

1703: Czar Peter the Great founds St. Petersburg as Russia's "window on the West." Major phase of southward and eastward Russian expansion under Peter and his successor Catherine.

1812: Napoleon burns Moscow, but loses an army on the way home.

1855–1861: Russia loses Crimean War and decides to modernize, including freeing the serfs.

1905: Russia loses a war with the Japanese, contributing to a failed revolution later glorified by the Communists as a manifestation of worker's consciousness.

1917: In March, the czar is ousted by a Provisional Government led by Aleksandr Kerensky.

1917: In November, the Provisional Government is ousted by the Bolsheviks (Communists), led by Lenin.

1924–1939:   Stalin purges the government and the army, and forced collectivization causes famine and tens of millions of deaths in Ukraine.

1939–1945:   World War II. Russia loses another 20 million to the Germans, but winds up with control over a sizable chunk of Eastern Europe.

1945–1962:   Peak of the Cold War. Russia acquires the atom bomb and launches the first satellite and the first manned space mission.

1970s: The "time of stagnation" under Leonid Brezhnev. The failure of the Communist economy becomes more and more apparent.

1985:   Mikhail Gorbachev comes to power and declares the beginning of *glasnost* (openness) and *perestroika* (restructuring).

1991:   Reactionaries try to topple Gorbachev. They fail to keep power, but so does Gorbachev. Boris Yeltsin takes control of the government and starts reforms.

1993:   Reactionaries try to topple Yeltsin. They fail to gain power, but Yeltsin is weakened.

1995–1996:   Boris Yeltsin hangs on to power despite grumbling from the ultra-nationalist right and the communist left.

Today: Stay tuned . . .

Baltic Timeline

1200–1300:   German merchants and clerics attempt respectively to colonize the Baltic states and Christianize their native populations. A German class of land-owning nobles emerges in Estonia and Latvia. Lithuania resists.

1386:   Preferring the Poles to the Germans, the Prince of Lithuania marries the Princess of Poland and unites the two countries. Catholicism becomes the state religion.

1520s: The Reformation reaches Estonia and Latvia.

1629: Sweden acquires most of Estonia and Latvia.

1700–1721: Russia wins Estonia and Latvia from Sweden in the Great Northern War.

1795: Lithuania becomes part of the Russian Empire in the third partition of Poland.

1850–1890: Independence movements start to roll. Ethnic and national consciousness grows in the Baltics.

1918–1921: The Baltics gain independence in the wake of the Russian Revolution and the First World War, but have to fight both the Germans and the Red Army for it. Ethnic Germans start leaving Estonia and Latvia.

1939: The secret Molotov–Ribbentrop pact between Hitler's Germany and Stalin's Russia declares the Baltic states part of Russia's sphere of influence.

1940–1945: The Baltics become a political football between Russia and Germany. Net result: mass deportations of Balts to Siberia and of Jews to the Nazi concentration camps, and the Soviet annexation of all three Baltic states.

1945–1989: Sovietization. Ethnic Russians move into the Baltics to take military and civilian jobs.

1989–1991: Under *glasnost*, a mass movement for an end to Soviet occupation and the restoration of independence gains steam. Lithuania declares independence first; Moscow's armed reprisals leave 14 dead in Vilnius.

August 1991: World recognition of Baltic independence comes in the wake of the failed coup in Moscow.

Let's Talk Telephones

In Europe, card-operated public phones are speedily replacing coin-operated phones. Each country sells telephone cards good for use in its country. Get a phone card at any post office. To make a call, pick up the receiver, insert your card in the slot in the phone, dial your number, make your call, then retrieve your card. The price of your call is automatically deducted from your card as you use it. If you have a phone card phobia, you'll usually find easy-to-use "talk now–pay later" metered phones in post offices. Avoid using hotel room phones, which are major rip-offs for anything other than local calls and calling-card calls.

Calling-Card Calls

Calling home is easy from any type of phone if you have an AT&T calling card. From a private phone, just dial the toll-free number to reach the operator. Using a public phone, first insert a small-value coin or a Russian or Baltic phone card. Then dial the operator, who will ask you for your calling-card number and place your call. Your bill awaits you at home (one more reason to prolong your vacation). For more information, see Introduction: Telephones and Mail.

AT&T's USA Direct Service

In ...	Dial ...
Moscow	755-5042
St. Petersburg	325-5042
Estonia	800-800-1001
Latvia	700-7007 (from 2-numbers or outside Riga area, dial 827-007-007)
Lithuania	8-(wait for tone)-196

Dialing Direct

Calling Between Countries: First dial the international access code, then the country code, followed by the area code, then the local number. In most of Europe, you dial the area code in full if you're calling within the country, but drop the initial zero when calling from outside the country, *though this does not apply to Russia & the Baltics—see Dialing Direct Within Russia and the Baltics, below.*

Calling Long Distance Within a Country: First dial the area code, then the local number.

Some of Europe's Exceptions: A few countries lack area codes, such as Denmark, Norway, and France; Latvia and Estonia are starting to follow this pattern too. You still use the above sequence and codes to dial, just skip the area code.

International Access Codes

When dialing direct, first dial the international access code of the country you're calling from.

Austria: 00	Latvia: 00
Belgium: 00	Lithuania: 810
Britain: 00	Netherlands: 00
Czech Republic: 00	Norway: 00
Denmark: 00	Portugal: 00
Estonia: 800	Russia: 810
Finland: 990	Spain: 07
France: 00	Sweden: 009
Germany: 00	Switzerland: 00
Ireland: 00	U.S.A./Canada: 011
Italy: 00	

Country Codes

After you've dialed the international access code, then dial the code of the country you're calling.

Austria: 43	Latvia: 371
Belgium: 32	Lithuania: 370
Britain: 44	Netherlands: 31
Czech Republic: 42	Norway: 47
Denmark: 45	Portugal: 351
Estonia: 372	Russia: 7
Finland: 358	Spain: 34
France: 33	Sweden: 46
Germany: 49	Switzerland: 41
Ireland: 353	U.S.A./Canada: 1
Italy: 39	

Dialing Direct Within Russia & the Baltics

The following table gives the sequence of numbers you dial when calling direct in Russia and the Baltics. "X" stands for any local telephone number listed in this book (including the initial "2" on some Tallinn and Riga numbers). So to dial local number 2/234-567 or 654-3210 in Tallinn from the U.S.A., dial 011-372-2234567 or 011-372-6543210. Baltic phone numbering is rapidly evolving, so remember that the information in this chart may change as well.

Dialing Direct Codes

From	To Moscow	St. Pete	Tallinn	Riga	Vilnius	U.S.A.
Moscow	—	8-812-x	8-014-x	8-013-x	8-012-2-x	8-10-1-x
St. Pete	8-095-x	—	8-014x	8-013-x	8-012-2-x	8-10-1-x
Tallinn	800-7-095-x	800-7-812-x	—	800-371-x	800-370-2-x	800-1-x
Riga*	00-7-095-x	00-7-812-x	00-372-x	—	00-370-2-x	00-1-x
Vilnius	810-7-095-x	810-7-812-x	810-372-x	810-371-x	—	8-10-1-x
U.S.A.	011-7-095-x	011-7-812-x	011-372-x	011-371-x	011-370-2-x	—

*From 7-numbers only. From 2-numbers, dial the same codes as from Moscow and St. Petersburg.

Metric Conversion (approximate)

1 inch = 25 millimeters
1 foot = 0.3 meter
1 yard = 0.9 meter
1 mile = 1.6 kilometers
1 centimeter = 0.4 inch
1 meter = 39.4 inches
1 kilometer = .62 mile

32 degrees F = 0 degrees C
82 degrees F = about 28 degrees C
1 ounce = 28 grams
1 kilogram = 2.2 pounds
1 quart = 0.95 liter
1 square yard = 0.8 square meter
1 acre = 0.4 hectare

Numbers and Stumblers

•Europeans write a few of their numbers differently than we do.1 = 1 4 = 4 , 7 = 7. Learn the difference or miss your train.
•In Europe, dates appear as day/month/year, so Christmas is 25-12-99.
•Commas are decimal points and decimals commas. A dollar and a half is 1,50 and there are 5.280 feet in a mile.
•When pointing, use your whole hand, palm downward.
•When counting with fingers, start with your thumb. If you hold up your first finger to request one item, you'll get two.

Climate

City	Jan	Mar	May	July	Sept	Nov
Average high/low temperatures (Fahrenheit) and average rainy days per month						
Helsinki/ Tallinn	26°/17° 20	32°/20° 14	56°/40° 12	71°/55° 14	59°/46° 15	37°/30° 19
Moscow	15°/3° 18	32°/18° 15	66°/46° 13	73°/55° 15	61°/45° 13	35°/26° 15
Riga/ Vilnius	25°/14° 19	35°/20° 16	61°/42° 13	71°/52° 12	63°/47° 17	39°/30° 19
St. Petersburg	19°/8° 21	32°/18° 14	59°/42° 13	70°/55° 13	60°/47° 17	35°/28° 18
Warsaw	32°/22° 15	42°/28° 11	67°/48° 11	75°/58° 16	66°/49° 12	42°/33° 12

- What we Americans call the second floor of a building is the first floor in Europe.
- Europeans keep the left "lane" open for passing on escalators and moving sidewalks. Keep to the right.

Public Holidays

Russia: Jan. 1 (New Year's), Jan. 7 (Christmas), March 8 (Women's Day), May 1, May 9 (Victory Day), June 12 (Independence Day), Dec. 31 (New Year's Eve).

Estonia: Jan. 1 (New Year's), Feb. 24 (Independence Day), May 1, (Good Friday, Easter), June 23 (Victory Day), June 24 (Midsummer), Nov. 16 (Rebirth Day), Dec. 25–26 (Christmas).

Latvia: Jan. 1 (New Year's), May 1, (Good Friday, Easter), June 23–24 (Midsummer), Nov. 18 (Independence Day), Dec. 25–26 (Christmas), Dec. 31 (New Year's Eve).

Lithuania: Jan. 1 (New Year's), Feb. 16 (Independence Day), May 1 (Good Friday, Easter, Sunday and Monday), July 6 (Statehood Day), Nov. 1 (All Saints), Dec. 25–26 (Christmas).

Learning Cyrillic

Russia uses the Cyrillic alphabet. If you spend 15 minutes learning it, you'll be able to read maps, street signs, food labels, subway directions, train schedules, menus, inscriptions, names of famous people, and Russian graffiti. Ignore Cyrillic, and you'll be completely unable to get around on public transportation, unable even to write the name of a destination for a taxi driver or train-ticket seller, unable to read a street sign, and totally reliant on English-speaking (hard cash–hungry) Russians. Tape this rip-out cheat sheet to the inside of your glasses. Chant it before going to sleep. Do whatever you need to do—just learn it. Also, some people don't realize that you can read Cyrillic words out loud. When you say Nevsky Prospekt, you're also saying Невский Проспект.

Cyrillic	English spelling	*Sounds like:*	Cyrillic	English spelling	*Sounds like:*
А а	a	*Ra*chm*a*ninoff	Т т	t	*T*urgenev
Б б	b	*B*aryshnikov	У у	u	*U*stinov
В в	v	Uncle *V*anya	Ф ф	f	*F*runze
Г г	g	*G*o*g*ol	Х х	kh	as in the
Д д	d	*D*ostoevski			Scottish lo*ch*
Е е	e	*Ye*ltsin	Ц ц	ts	*Ts*arevich
Ё ё	yo	*Yo*ssarian	Ч ч	ch	T*ch*aikovsky
Ж ж	zh	Bre*zh*nev	Ш ш	sh	Pu*sh*kin
З з	z	*Z*amiatin	Щ щ	shch	Khru*shch*ev
И и	i	*I*zvesti*y*a	Ъ ъ	—	"hard sign"
Й й	i	Tolsto*y*			(ignore it)
К к	k	*C*atherine	Ы ы	y	Solzhenits*y*n
Л л	l	*L*enin	Ь ь	—	"soft sign"
М м	m	*M*olotov			(ignore it)
Н н	n	*N*abokov	Э э	e	*E*thelred the
О о	o	*O*blomov			Unre*a*dy
П п	p	*P*asternak	Ю ю	yu	*Yu*goslavia
Р р	r	*R*asputin	Я я	ya	*Ya*lta
С с	s	*S*uvorov			

Survival Phrases

In the following list, pronounce *a* as in car, *e* as in bet, *i* as in spaghetti, *o* as in more, *u* as in tune. In Estonian, ä, ö, and ü have the same sounds as umlauts in German (*ä* is like the English *a* in cat; for *ö* and *ü*, try to say "e" with your lips rounded).

English	Estonian	Latvian	Lithuanian	Russian
yes	**ya**	yā	**taip**	da
no	**ei**	nē	**ne**	nyet
hello	**te*re***	*lab*dien	***la*ba *di*ena**	*zdra*sstvuy-tye
goodbye	**head *ae*ga**	*vi*suga*i*shu	***vi*so gero**	do svid*a*nya
please	***pa*lun**	*lu*dzu	***pra*shom**	paz*hal*sta
thank you	**tänan**	*pal*dies	***a*chu**	spa*si*ba
excuse me	***va*bandage**	*at*vainoyiet	**atsipras*hau***	izvi*ni*tye
one	**üks**	viens	***vi*enas**	a*din*
two	**kaks**	divs	**du**	dva
three	**kolm**	tris	**tris**	tri
Where is...?	**Kus on...?**	Kur ir...?	**Kur...?**	Gdye...?
How much?	**Kui *pal*yu *mak*sab?**	Tsik *mak*sā?	**Kiek *kai*nuoya?**	*Skol*ka sto*y*it?
I don't understand	**Ma ei sa *a*ru**	Es *ne*saprotu	**Ash *ne*su*pran*tu**	Nye *po*nil
Do you speak English?	**Kas te*ie* räägite *in*glise keelt?**	*Vai* jūs ru*nā*jet-*an*gliski?	**Ar *kal*bates *an*glishkai?**	Vi gava*ri*-tye pa an*gli*ski?

Buying Train Tickets

Please help me to buy the following tickets:
Пожалуйста; помагите мене купить эти билеты:

Destination/До станции _____
Month/Месяц: _____   Date/Число: _____
Train number/Поезд Nr _____
Departure time/Отправление в _____

Number of passengers/Количество человек: _____
Class/Тип: 2-berth/СВ
4-berth/купейный
Sitting place/Сиденный

Surname(s)/Фамипия: _____
Citizenship/Гражданство: _____

Нет мест.
There are no seats available.

Мест ест; но в другом классе.
There are seats, but only in a different class.

Здесь не продаём.
We don't sell these tickets at this window.

Faxing Your Hotel Reservation

Most hotel managers know basic "hotel English." Faxing is the preferred method for reserving a room. It's more accurate and cheaper than telephoning and much faster than writing a letter. Use this handy form for your fax. Photocopy and fax away.

One-Page Fax

To: _____ @ _____
        hotel   *fax*

From: _____ @ _____
        name   *fax*

Today's date: ____ /_____ /____
                    day   *month*   *year*

Dear Hotel _____,

Please make this reservation for me:

Name: _____

Total # of people: _____   # of rooms: _____   # of nights: _____

Arriving: ____ /_____ /____ My time of arrival (24-hr clock): _____
            day *month* *year* (I will telephone if I will be late)

Departing: ____ /_____ /____
              day *month* *year*

Room(s): Single___ Double___ Twin___ Triple___ Quad___

With: Toilet___ Shower___ Bath___ Sink only___

Special needs: View___ Quiet___ Cheapest Room___

Credit card: Visa___ MasterCard___ American Express___

Card #: _____

Expiration Date:_____

Name on card: _____

You may charge me for the first night as a deposit. Please fax or mail me confirmation of my reservation, along with the type of room reserved, the price, and whether the price includes breakfast. Thank you.

_____
Signature

_____
Name

_____
Address

_____
City   *State*   *Zip Code*   *Country*

Road Scholar Feedback for Russia and the Baltics

We're all in the same travelers' school of hard knocks. Your feedback helps us improve this guidebook for future travelers. Please fill this out (attach more info or any tips/favorite discoveries if you like) and send it to us. As thanks for your help, we'll send you our quarterly travel newsletter free for one year. Thanks! **Rick**

I traveled mainly by: ___ Car   ___ Train/bus tickets
___ Railpass   Other (please list _____)

Number of people traveling together:
___ Solo   ___ 2   ___ 3   ___ 4   ___ Over 4   ___ Tour

Ages of traveler/s (including children):

_____

I visited _____countries in _____weeks.

I traveled in: ___ Spring ___ Summer ___ Fall ___ Winter

My daily budget per person (excluding transportation):
___ Under $40   ___ $40–$60   ___ $60–$80   ___ $80–$120
___ over $120   ___ Don't know

Average cost of hotel rooms: Single room $_____
Double room $_____   Other (type _____) $_____

Favorite tip from this book:

_____

Biggest waste of time or money caused by this book:

_____

Other Rick Steves books used for this trip:

_____

Hotel listings from this book should be geared toward places that are:
___Cheaper   ___More expensive   ___About the same

Of the recommended accommodations/restaurants used, which was:

Best _____

    Why? _____

Worst _____

    Why? _____

I reserved rooms:

____from USA   ____in advance as I traveled

____same day by phone   ____just showed up

Getting rooms in recommended hotels was:

____easy   ____mixed   ____frustrating

Of the sights/experiences/destinations recommended by this book, which was:

Most overrated _____

    Why? _____

Most underrated _____

    Why? _____

Best ways to improve this book:

_____

I'd like a free newsletter subscription:

___ Yes   ___ No   ___ Already on list

_____

Name

_____

Address

_____

City, State, Zip

_____

E-mail Address

Please send to:
ETBD • Box 2009, Edmonds, WA 98020

INDEX

Rick Steves' Phrase Books

Unlike other phrase books and dictionaries on the market, my well-tested phrases and key words cover every situation a traveler is likely to encounter. With these books you'll laugh with your cabby, disarm street thieves with insults, and charm new European friends.

Each book in the series is 4" x 6", with maps.

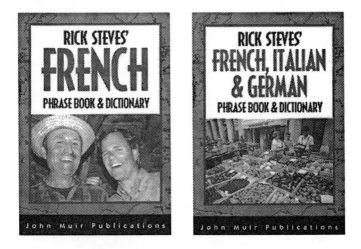

RICK STEVES' FRENCH PHRASE BOOK & DICTIONARY
U.S. $5.95/Canada $8.50

RICK STEVES' GERMAN PHRASE BOOK & DICTIONARY
U.S. $5.95/Canada $8.50

RICK STEVES' ITALIAN PHRASE BOOK & DICTIONARY
U.S. $5.95/Canada $8.50

RICK STEVES' SPANISH & PORTUGUESE PHRASE BOOK & DICTIONARY
U.S. $7.95/Canada $11.25

RICK STEVES' FRENCH, ITALIAN & GERMAN PHRASE BOOK & DICTIONARY
U.S. $7.95/Canada $11.25

Books from John Muir Publications